Stuart Yarnold

Poker for Seniors

For the Over 50s

In easy steps is an imprint of In Easy Steps Limited
Southfield Road · Southam
Warwickshire CV47 0FB · United Kingdom
www.ineasysteps.com

Notice of Liability
Every effort has been made to ensure that this book
contains accurate and current information. However, In
Easy Steps Limited and the author shall not be liable for
any loss or damage suffered by readers as a result of
any information contained herein.

Trademarks
All trademarks are acknowledged as belonging to their
respective companies.

Printed and bound in the United Kingdom

ISBN 978-1-84078-375-9

Contents

1 Playing Options 7

Introduction	8
Where to Play	9
Casinos	9
Dedicated Poker Rooms	10
Online	10
Poker Parties	11

2 Choosing Your Poker Game and Table 15

Choosing the Right Game	16
No-Limit Games	16
Pot-Limit Games	17
Fixed-Limit Games	17
Choosing the Right Table	18
Average Pot Versus Stack	18
Quality of the Opposition	19
Relative Table Position	20
Identifying Dangerous Opponents	21
Identifying Weak Opponents	22
Number of Opponents	22

3 Texas Hold'em – The Basics 23

How to Play Texas Hold'em	24
Poker Hand Rankings	26
Poker Hand Values	27
Hand Elements	31
Drawing Hands	33
Table Position	34
Playing Styles	36
Tells	37
Inside the Mind of a Pro	38

4   Poker Ploys   39

Playing the Percentages	40
Pot Odds	41
Hand Odds	41
Raising	44
Check-Raising	46
Slow-Playing	46
Bluffing	47
Deception	49

5   Fixed-Limit Texas Hold'em Strategy   51

Start Cards	52
Pre-Flop Play	53
Playing From the Blinds	57
Common Pre-Flop Mistakes	59
Playing the Flop	60
Playing Pairs on the Flop	62
Two Pairs on the Flop	64
Playing Sets on the Flop	66
Flush Draws on the Flop	68
Straight Draws on the Flop	70
Drawing Hands/Pot Odds	72
Playing a Flush or Straight on the Flop	73
Overcards on the Flop	74
Full House on the Flop	75
Playing the Turn	76
Playing the River	77
Short-Hand Play	78
Texas Hold'em Odds	79

6   No-Limit Texas Hold'em Strategy   81

Introduction	82
Start Cards	83
Pre-Flop Strategy	84
Post-Flop Strategy	87
The All-In Bet	88

Bluffing   89
Trapping   90
Stack Size   91
Common No-Limit Mistakes   92

7   Online Poker   93

Live Versus Online   94
Online Poker Software   96
Cashing In   97
Bonuses   98
Pros & Cons of Online Poker   100
Three Top Poker Rooms   102

8   Omaha   105

Introduction   106
Evaluating Your Start Cards   108
Playable Start Cards   110
Low-Hand Qualification   115
Pre-Flop Strategy   116
Reading the Board   117
Counterfeiting   118
Playing the Flop   119
The Turn and the River   122
Common Omaha Mistakes   124

9   Seven-Card Stud   125

Seven-Card Stud – the Rules   126
Factors Specific to Seven-Card Stud   128
Start Cards   130
Playing Pairs   131
Playing Sets   134
Playing Two Pairs   137
Playing Flush Draws   139
Playing Straight Draws   141
Playing Killer Hands   143

10 Tournaments — 145

Introduction	146
Types of Tournament	147
Prize Money	151
Chip Stacks	152
Multi-Table Strategy	154
Single-Table Strategy	157
Heads-Up Strategy	159

11 Improving Your Game — 161

Practice, Practice, Practice	162
Poker Simulation Software	163
Keep Records	164
Analyze Your Game	165
Poker Analysis Software	165
How to Avoid Going on Tilt	166

12 Miscellaneous Poker Topics — 167

Other Poker Games	168
How Much Can You Win?	169
Handling Winning & Losing Streaks	170
The World Series of Poker (WSOP)	172
Cheating	174
Poker Resources	176

Glossary — 177

Index — 187

1 Playing Options

We start with a brief look at the various places where you can play poker, and see the pros and cons of each.

8 Introduction

9 Where to Play

9 Casinos

10 Dedicated Poker Rooms

10 Online

11 Poker Parties

Introduction

So, you made it! Retirement has finally arrived and you're now officially old. No more getting up at 6.30am and battling through rush-hour traffic to get to work. No longer do you have to be nice to people you'd rather not be nice to. Now, at last, you can please yourself and do just what you want to.

Of course, you may not be a senior citizen at all, you may just have time on your hands at certain times of the day and need some way of filling it.

Whichever applies to you, the question is what are you going to do? You can take up a hobby such as fishing or woodwork. You can sit down and write that novel you always wanted to but could never find the time for. Well, here's another suggestion – how about playing poker.

Poker is one of the most fascinating of all the card games and, if played well, can be extremely rewarding. Not only can you while away many hours enjoyably playing this game, you can also make serious money at it. Win or lose, it has other advantages as well. For example, poker requires concentration, thought and discipline, all qualities that old people tend to lose. If nothing else, playing poker regularly will keep your mind sharp and alert.

This book has been written for people just like you – people who would like to give poker a try but don't know where to begin. It won't make you an expert – only experience and dedication can do that – but by the time you reach the last page, you will already be a better player than most.

We concentrate on the most popular variant of poker – Texas Hold'em, and also give you a good grounding in Omaha and Seven-Card Stud. Plus, you will learn about poker tournaments, which is where really serious money can be won. No poker book these days would be complete without a mention of online poker (which provides many advantages to the senior citizen). You will find this here as well.

Hot tip

You can take the game of poker as far as you want. Most will see it as no more than an interesting diversion. However, if you are determined enough, you can become extremely proficient and make a lot of money.

Where to Play

Having decided to give it a go, your first decision is where to play. Here, you have four options: 1) casinos, 2) dedicated poker rooms, c) online and d) poker parties.

Casinos

The first thing to say here is that unless you live near to a really large casino, the chances are that your options will be very limited. In the average casino, the emphasis is more on Roulette, Blackjack and Slot Machines as these produce far more profit for the casino operator than does poker.

The reason for this is that in poker, the casino's profit comes from the rake. This is a percentage (typically 10 to 15%) taken from each pot. Furthermore, there is usually a cap on the rake that prevents the casino taking a disproportionate amount from any one pot. For example, 15% of a $2000 pot is $300; however, due to the cap, the casino will take a much smaller amount. Therefore, the games mentioned above make much more for the casino.

As a result, in most casinos, there may only be one or two poker tables. Usually, you will have to wait a considerable amount of time before a seat becomes available at one.

Another problem for the beginner (who should only be playing at the low-limits) is that casinos aren't interested in the low profits that low-limit tables generate. Thus, you may find yourself playing for stakes that are too high for your level of expertise and experience.

Playing at a live poker table can also be an intimidating experience for the beginner. Make a foolish mistake and you are going to feel foolish.

However, at the very large casinos, such as the ones you will find in Las Vegas and Atlantic City, there will be many tables at both high and low limits. Some of these casinos also provide free poker lessons, which are an invaluable introduction not only to the mechanics of playing poker but also to playing it in a live casino.

Beware

If you are new to this game, do not sit down at a table unless you are comfortable with the table stakes.

Don't forget

If you get the opportunity, take advantage of the free poker lessons offered in the larger casinos.

...cont'd

Dedicated Poker Rooms

If you live in a city or near one, the chances are that you will find an establishment dedicated to poker and nothing else.

The big advantage these provide is choice. There will be a good number of tables available and at various limits, which should enable you to find a game commensurate with your ability and experience.

In all other respects, however, it will be little different than playing in a casino.

Online

The Internet has fuelled the biggest surge ever seen in the game of poker simply by making it instantly available to anyone who owns a computer. Millions of people are now playing who would never have even considered it previously.

We cover the subject of online poker in some depth in Chapter 7 so won't go into it too much here. Briefly, though, it offers many advantages over the traditional casino or poker room.

Instant availability, as we've already mentioned, is one. Moreover, it's available 24 hours a day, seven days a week. Convenience is another – with an appropriate setup, you can play from simply anywhere. This is particularly handy for the elderly or infirm who would find it difficult, or even impossible, to travel to a casino.

Mention must also be made of the fact that online poker rooms offer much better value than their land-based counterparts. The rake taken by the latter is typically in the region of 10 to 15%; online poker rooms, however, rarely take more than 5%. For regular players, this can add up to literally thousands of dollars saved over a period.

There's also the issue of choice. Online poker rooms offer dozens, even hundreds of tables from the micro-limits up to high-roller limits. Live poker rooms simply cannot match this.

Hot tip

Another advantage of online poker for the advanced player is being able to play several tables at once.

Poker Parties

For those who just like the occasional game and have no desire to play in a casino or online, the poker party is the perfect solution.

These are usually as much a social event as a game of poker and can be great fun. So let's see what you need to set up a poker party.

You can of course simply sit around the coffee table with 3 or 4 pals, a box of matchsticks and a dog-eared pack of cards. However, apart from not doing your back any good, this is not going to be much of an experience. How authentic you want your party to be will depend on how much you're prepared to spend and how much trouble you're prepared to go to.

We'll start with a cheap and cheerful setup. The first thing you'll need will be a decent pack of plastic-coated cards. These are much nicer to handle than cheaper linen ones.

Then you'll need something to play on. The cheapest option here is a printed poker table cover. Simply spread it over a suitably sized table and, hey presto, you've got something that resembles a poker table. Another, slightly more expensive, option is a solid foldable cover, as shown below:

Hot tip

If you want the ultimate poker party, there are companies that will supply a professional poker table, a skilled dealer and all the accessories (all you have to do is win enough to pay for it all).

11

...cont'd

The next requisite is a set of chips. Chip sets are available in various sizes (number of chips) and denominations, so make sure you get one that a) provides enough chips for the number of players you will have and, b) has suitable denominations for the stakes you will be playing at. It's no good having chips that range from $10 to $1000 if you're only playing for low-limit stakes.

Hot tip

The best quality poker chips are made from clay and give a satisfying chink. Cheaper ones are plastic and sound like they are.

Apart from the beer and nibbles, that's all you need for a basic poker party. If you want something better, however, read on.

With regard to authenticity, the table is the most important factor. So instead of settling for a simple table cover, you can buy a proper poker table. Here, again, you have various options.

Hot tip

For most people, a fold-away table will be the best option as they can be put away when not in use.

If space is an issue, you can opt for a simple fold-away table, which can be brought out only when required. You can also buy poker tables with a reversible top. These will serve as a dining table with the top one way, and a poker table with the top reversed.

Poker table with fold-away legs

If you've got a couple of thousand dollars to spare, you can buy a table that is as near to the ones you'd find in a casino as makes no difference. An example is shown below:

Having acquired a decent table, you will now need to add some poker accessories to it. First in the list is a shuffling shoe. Not only does this eliminate the possibility of the dealer cheating, if you get an automatic model this will speed the game up considerably.

Hot tip

Cheating can be an issue in home poker games. By using an automatic shuffling shoe, the possibility of the dealer cheating is much reduced.

...cont'd

If you're planning on holding a tournament, you might also consider buying a tournament director. While not essential, you will find that a director is a great aid. It can be a program running from a laptop or PC strategically placed where all the players can see it, or a hardware device that sits on the table itself.

Tournament directors simplify the procedure of setting up a tournament considerably by enabling you to set the parameters of the tournament. For example: stakes, number of blinds periods, length of the blind periods, break periods, etc. For a comprehensive list of poker terms, please see the Glossary, p177–186.

In operation, all this information is displayed by the director so that players know exactly what is going on. It will also issue audible alerts when a blind period is finished.

The Tournament Director - *sample.tdt		
Texas Freeze Out		
$50.00 Buy-in, $50.00 to Rebuy (Through Round 6, Max 1 per player), No Add-ons		

Round 1	**7:04**	Next Break 57:04
Entries 45		Chip Leaders
Players In 45		Aaron P $2,215
		Andrew C $2,100
		Andrew T $1,875
Rebuys 0	No Limit Texas Hold 'Em	Andrew D $1,800
		Brent F $1,700
		Brian S $1,650
Chip Count $67,500	**Blinds**	William P $1,500
	$10 / $20	Corey C $1,500
Avg Stack $1,500		Clay L $1,500
		Chris G $1,500
Total Pot $2,250.00	Next Round: No Limit Texas Hold 'Em	Carlos A $1,500
	Blinds: $15 / $30	Craig T $1,200

1st Place: $905 2nd Place: $515 3rd Place: $290 4th Place: $225
5th Place: $180 6th Place: $135

Screenshot from a software director, and a hardware director

2 Choosing Your Poker Game and Table

It's very important to play the right game at the right table. This is particularly so for novices, for whom the wrong choice can be devastating. Here, we look at all the factors you need to consider in order to find a profitable table.

16 Choosing the Right Game

16 No-Limit Games

17 Pot-Limit Games

17 Fixed-Limit Games

18 Choosing the Right Table

18 Average Pot Versus Stack

19 Quality of the Opposition

20 Relative Table Position

21 Identifying Dangerous Opponents

22 Identifying Weak Opponents

22 Number of Opponents

Choosing the Right Game

Throughout the next five chapters we are going to concentrate on Texas Hold'em. Poker rooms offer three variations of this game: fixed-limit, no-limit and pot-limit. The rules are the same for each; the difference lies in the betting structure. For the beginner, making the correct choice here is crucial, and this section will show you why.

No-Limit Games

No-limit poker means just what the name implies – you can bet whatever you like up to the amount in front of you. Because of this, it is possible to lose your entire stack in a single hand if you make the wrong call. The following example illustrates the danger of this type of game.

You sit down with $20 at a $0.50/1.00 no-limit table. After two hours you're up to $75 and things are looking good.

Then it happens. You hit an ace set (three aces) and raise by $15. All your opponents fold with the exception of Player A who re-raises by $20. You respond by calling; now you have $35 in the pot. On the next round of betting, you bet $10 and player A raises you by $30. To see A's cards, you now have to go all-in (see bottom margin note).

You have three aces, which is a very good hand but not one that's unbeatable. If you call, you have a good chance of winning. If you lose, though, you will have lost your entire stack in one hand. If you fold, you lose the $45 you have already staked. The former is a catastrophe, the latter is a minor catastrophe. An even bigger catastrophe, however, will be folding the winning hand. In this case, you'll have lost a pot that's worth well over $100.

This is a tricky situation and demands that you get your next move right. An experienced player will know how to handle the dilemma. A beginner, though, will probably chicken out and take the easy option of folding, which could well be a major mistake. It's better not to get yourself involved in this type of scenario at all by avoiding no-limit to begin with.

Beware

The action at no-limit tables is fast and furious, and it is possible to win (and lose) a lot of money very quickly. For these reasons, many good poker players play no-limit exclusively. For the inexperienced player, they are a minefield that should be given a wide berth.

Hot tip

All-in is when a player puts his or her entire stack in the pot.

Pot-Limit Games

Pot-limit games are very similar to no-limit games. The only difference is that players can bet no more than the amount in the pot. For example, say there is $20 in the pot after one round of betting. The player opening the second round may bet any amount up to $20. If he or she does bet $20, making a pot of $40, the next player may call the first player's bet ($20) and then raise the amount of the current pot, including the call ($60), for a total bet of $80.

In the early betting rounds, therefore, where the pot will be small, the danger of being faced with a monster bet to stay in the game is much reduced. However, in a game where the betting is heavy, the pot size will increase rapidly and, consequently, so will the maximum bet allowed.

For the beginner, the dangers inherent in pot-limit poker are much the same as in no-limit. It should, therefore, be avoided initially.

Fixed-Limit Games

In fixed-limit poker, all bet sizes are predetermined. For example, all bets during the first two rounds of a $5.00/10.00 Texas Hold'em game are in increments of $5 ($5 being the minimum bet). If player A bets $5 then player B can fold, call for $5, or raise to $10. In the last two betting rounds, the minimum bet is $10 and bets rise in increments of $10.

Something else to be aware of is that most poker rooms limit the number of raises during any betting round in fixed-limit Texas Hold'em to four. This includes a bet, raise, re-raise, and cap. The cap is the third and final raise. After a betting round is capped, players still in the hand only have the option to call or to fold.

These games are much safer for the beginner as there is no danger of being faced with a huge bet. Therefore, fixed-limit games are the ones recommended for those new to the game of poker.

Hot tip

Novices are advised to start at fixed-limit tables as the risk of sustaining heavy losses in a short period is much less.

17

Hot tip

All poker professionals will tell you that good table choice is very important. If they think this then so should you.

Beware

Do not sit down at a table with a stack that is not big enough to take full advantage of good hands.

Choosing the Right Table

Experienced players consider several factors before sitting down at a table. This is because they know that if they pick the right one, their chances of walking away with a pocketful of cash at the end of the session will be substantially higher.

If good players feel the need to do this, then it is even more imperative that beginners do the same. However, they rarely do, which is just one of the many reasons that these players usually lose when they first start playing.

So before you place your chips on a table, we are going to show how to choose one at which you have a good chance of winning.

Average Pot Versus Stack

You must have an adequate amount of money (your stack) in relation to the average pot at the table. For example, if you sit down with $10 at a table where the average pot is $50, you are likely to experience the following:

First, you may hit a monster hand at the same time that two other players also get good hands that they are prepared to commit their chips to. Because you only have $10, you will be all-in very early in the game. Meanwhile, the others will continue to bet in another pot. When the showdown comes, although you've got the best hand, you will only win the pot (side pot) that you were involved in. The other pot (that contains most of the money) will go to the player with the next best hand. You will have missed an opportunity to win a huge pot.

Second, in an effort to avoid busting-out, you will play ultra-cautiously. In doing so, you may well pass up good winning opportunities. In other words, you're compromising yourself.

Third, your opponents will play differently against you. They will try to take advantage by calling and raising your bets, knowing you haven't got enough to hurt them if you do win a hand.

All no-limit tables have a minimum and maximum buy-in amount. For example: $20 minimum, $100 maximum. Ideally, you would sit down with the maximum amount – $100.

At fixed-limit tables, however, while there is a minimum buy-in, there is no maximum amount. The reason for this is that because bets are fixed, players with large stacks have no "power" advantage over those who don't.

Quality of the Opposition

This is the most important factor of all. Quite simply, if you get this right you should win; get it wrong and you'll probably lose. You can determine this as follows:

Before joining a table, watch how the hands are being played. What you are looking for is a table with several players who bet on most hands. Even better are players who are constantly raising. The latter are usually betting on mediocre hands and will try and bluff their way out of trouble by raising again. Play the right strategy against players of this type and you will beat them. Tight players who fold most hands are no-risk types who will be more difficult to beat.

If you're playing at an online poker room, a quicker way of establishing how "tight" or "loose" a table is can be found in the poker room's lobby. An example from Poker Stars is shown below:

Hot tip

If you find yourself becoming short-stacked, top it up. You must keep it at a level that will enable you to make the most of situations where you have the best hand.

Hot tip

In poker, the term "tight" is used to describe players who play very cautiously. A "loose" player is the opposite: one who plays recklessly.

All	High	Medium		Low		Micro	
Table	Stakes ▼	Limit	Plrs	Wait	Avg Pot	Plrs/Flop	H/hr
Forsytia	$0.10/$0.25	PL	3		$1	29%	66
Geldonia	$0.10/$0.25	PL	3		$4	75%	81
Rana IV	$0.10/$0.25	PL	3		$0.81	44%	128
Sichuan	$0.10/$0.25	PL	3		$1	69%	124
Baade III	$0.10/$0.25	NL	4		$2	64%	70
Balios II (fast)	$0.10/$0.25	NL	4		$6	25%	105
Devosa	$0.10/$0.25	NL	4		$3	63%	120
Luisa	$0.10/$0.25	NL	4		$2	50%	144
Eduarda III	$0.10/$0.25	NL	5		$4	61%	76
Lacerta IV (fast)	$0.10/$0.25	NL	5		$1	29%	116
Nipponia	$0.10/$0.25	NL	5		$1	35%	138
Soomana IV (fast)	$0.10/$0.25	NL	5		$1	48%	97
Penthesilea	$0.10/$0.25	NL	6		$2	39%	112
Ursina (fast)	$0.10/$0.25	NL	6		$2	9%	105
Corvus	$0.10/$0.25	NL	7	2	$4	41%	57

...cont'd

Look at the Plrs/Flop column, which will tell you the percentage of the players who bet through to the flop (the first three community cards). The higher this figure, the looser, and potentially more profitable, the table will be. In our example, we have highlighted a table where the percentage is 69. Play the correct strategy here, and with an average run of the cards you should do well.

Relative Table Position

The choice of where to position yourself at the table is not as important as the selection of the table itself, but still shouldn't be overlooked. You are said to have position on your opponents if they are seated on your right – you act after they do. Therefore, you want your stronger opponents on your right. Usually, this means tight players – those that are very choosy about which hands they choose to play.

With regard to loose players, you want to try to get any maniacs (those that love to bet with very little to back it up) on your immediate left. This presents you with several advantages:

- First, you will be able to see how every other player after the maniac reacts to his/her betting

- Second, you'll be able to use the maniac as an unwitting partner to knock out the players after him or her. If, for example, you hit a top pair and raise, the maniac may well re-raise, making it too costly for the others to chase their straight and flush draws

- Third, a maniac enables you to be deceptive. Let's say you hit a three-of-a-kind. You check (which suggests you have a weak hand) to the maniac who bets. Everyone knows the maniac has probably got nothing and will call if they have a half-decent hand. When the betting gets round to you again, you can now raise with plenty of money already in the pot

Don't forget

It's a big advantage to have tight players on your immediate right because these players will only raise when they hold a top hand. Because you act after them, you have the opportunity to fold a marginal hand that you might otherwise have bet on.

Identifying Dangerous Opponents

Basically, there are two types of players who are dangerous. The first, not surprisingly, is the poker professional who plays to a strategy, works out the opposition, knows the percentages, and cannot be bullied out of a pot. These players can be hard to identfy as such because they also know how to disguise their strategy by mixing up their play.

In general, though, the top-notch poker player plays a tight/aggressive game. This means usually playing only the top start cards but playing them extremely aggressively. So when you are watching a table to see if it's suitable, and you see players who fold most of the time but raise aggressively when they do play, you can put them down as opponents to be careful with. If you do sit down at the table, avoid any confrontations with them unless you are holding a very good hand.

The second type is the maniac and they are very easy to spot. These people play literally every hand and will often raise and re-raise right down to the river. Most of the time they lose, but now and again (and this is why they're dangerous) they get lucky. The problem with them is that it's impossible to have any idea of what they have. Usually it's nothing, but because they can't be intimidated by a raise, it's impossible to prevent them playing speculative hands. You can have them beaten as far as the final card, but if they get lucky and the right card falls for them, all of a sudden their second-best hand becomes a winning one. The following is a typical example:

You're playing no-limit and have A-K. The maniac has the six and three of diamonds. The flop cards are the queen of diamonds, jack of spades and ten of hearts. You therefore have an A-K-Q-J-T straight, while the maniac has nothing other than an outside chance of a diamond flush. With such a good hand you put in a big raise and at this point any sensible player would fold.

Beware

When the cards are falling for them, maniacs can make a big dent in your stack.

...cont'd

However, the maniac is not called a maniac for nothing. Your raise is called and the turn card is another diamond. You go all-in, and still the maniac calls. The final card is yet another diamond and you're beaten by a flush. You've had the best hand all the way, you've played it correctly, and against any other type of player you would have won. While you should be able to get your money back from the maniac in subsequent hands, you need to be wary with this kind of player.

Identifying Weak Opponents

Commonly known as "fish" in poker parlance, weak players are what any good player is looking for. Finding a table swimming with fish is a dream come true. Look for the following:

- Players who play too many hands. While we have already mentioned this, it bears repeating. Players who do this just cannot win – it's statistically impossible

- Maniacs who persist in playing to the river in the hope of catching a lucky card. Finding one of these is the poker equivalent of stumbling across a gold mine. Just bear in mind that you can come unstuck against them occasionally

- Players who are losing consistently. They may not be bad players, but just down on their luck. Have no pity though, you must take advantage

Number of Opponents

Quite simply, the more opponents you have, the less chance you have of winning any given hand. Because there are so many opponents to beat, playing ten-seaters requires a lot of patience and self-discipline – you have to wait for good cards. At six-seaters, however, you will have to play a greater range of hands. For example, at a ten-seater A-J unsuited is usually a folding hand, but at a six-seater it is a calling, or even a raising hand, depending on table position.

Beware

In general, we do not recommend that beginners play at six-seat tables. The action is a lot faster and this tends to attract the better players.

Hot tip

"Fish" is poker parlance for really bad players.

3 Texas Hold'em – The Basics

This chapter explains the rules, hand rankings, and the relative value of the various hands. Also, hand elements, such as kickers, what a drawing hand is, and terms such as inside straight and flush draw.

24 How to Play Texas Hold'em

26 Poker Hand Rankings

27 Poker Hand Values

31 Hand Elements

33 Drawing Hands

34 Table Position

36 Playing Styles

37 Tells

38 Inside the Mind of a Pro

How to Play Texas Hold'em

Texas Hold'em is the most popular of the various poker games, the extensive television coverage it receives probably being the main reason. Another is the fact that it is one of the easier variations of poker to learn and can be picked up in a few minutes by anyone.

Rules of Texas Hold'em

At the beginning of each hand, the two players to the left of the dealer button each place a predetermined stake into the pot. These two stakes are known as the *blinds*, and the act of placing them is known as *posting the blinds*. The player immediately to the left of the dealer posts the *small blind* and the next player on the left posts the *big blind*. The small blind is set at half (rounded down to the nearest dollar) of the table's lower limit, e.g. at a $5.00/10.00 table, it will be $2. The big blind is set at the lower limit and so will be $5.

Once the blinds have been posted, two cards are dealt face-down to the players. Each player will be able to see their own cards but not those of their opponents. These cards are known as the start, hole or pocket cards.

The first round of betting now commences: this stage of the game is known as the *pre-flop*. The first player to bet is the one immediately to the left of the two players who posted the blinds. The amount of money that can be bet depends on whether the game is a fixed-limit, pot-limit, or no-limit game. As with all forms of poker, players have options to fold, check, call or raise.

When the round of betting has finished, the dealer deals three cards face-up (known as community or board cards) in the middle of the table where they can be seen by all the players. This procedure is known as *dealing the flop*, and the three flop cards are used by each player to make the best hand in conjunction with their start cards.

Hot tip

Note that the blinds count towards the first bets of the players who posted them. For example, if you posted a small blind of $2 at a $5.00/10.00 table, the other players have to bet at least $5. On your first bet, however, you only have to bet $3 as you have already bet $2. From then on, you have to bet the same minimum amount as the others.

Hot tip

The dealer button passes to each player in turn. The player to the left of the big blind (third from the dealer button) is the first to make a move when the betting starts.

While there are still two more cards to come, at this stage of the game players will have a good idea of the potential strength of their hand, and whether it's worth persevering with it. Note that a common mistake made by inexperienced players at this point is continuing with hands that have little realistic prospect of winning. Once in a while they will get lucky and hit a good card on the turn or river but, more often than not, they won't and will lose. Judging which hands have a good chance of winning is a basic and very important part of playing poker.

A second round of betting now takes place, starting with the player to the left of the dealer (the small blind). When the round of betting has finished, the dealer deals a fourth face-up communal card. This is known as the turn card.

Starting with the player to the left of the dealer button, another round of betting begins. At the end of this, a final community card is dealt, making a total of five. This is known as the river card.

Assuming you are still in the game, you now have the five community cards and your two start cards with which to make a hand. Typically, by this stage most of the players will have folded. The players remaining will have either hit their hand, or missed it.

A final round of betting takes place, after which all the players remaining in the game reveal their hands. This begins with the player to the left of the last player to call and is known as the showdown. The player with the best hand wins the pot, minus the poker room's rake.

The next game now starts with the dealer button advancing one place to the left. The player who posted the big blind in the previous game now has to post the small blind. The big blind passes to the next player on the left. In this way all the players are obliged to place money in the pot every few hands.

Hot tip

The player who opens a betting round determines whether the check option will be available to the other players. If the player checks then the next player can also check and so on. However, if a player bets instead of checking, the check option will not be available to the players who follow.

Poker Hand Rankings

Having learned the rules of Texas Hold'em, the next thing you need to know is the range of hands that can be made. The following table lists them in order of ranking.

Royal Flush	Ace, king, queen, jack, and ten, all of the same suit. This is the best hand possible – in the unlikely event of you ever getting one, pray somebody else also has a good hand and is prepared to go all the way with it
Straight Flush	Five cards of consecutive rank, all of the same suit. It's very rare to see one of these
Four-of-a-Kind (known as quads)	Four cards of any one rank, and any other card. This hand pops up occasionally and is almost a guaranteed winner
Full House	Three cards of one rank, and two cards of another rank. An excellent hand with which you'd be very unlucky to lose. (It does happen occasionally, though)
Flush	Any five cards of the same suit. A very strong hand that will usually win
Straight	Five cards of consecutive rank. A strong hand that usually wins
Three-of-a-Kind (known as a set, or trips)	Three cards of the same rank and two unrelated cards. A good hand but often beaten by flushes and straights
Two Pairs	Two cards of one rank, two cards of another rank, and an unrelated fifth card. A reasonable hand that wins many pots
Pair	Two cards of the same rank, and three other unrelated cards. A weak hand that loses more often than not
High Card	Five unrelated cards – no pair, no flush, no straight – nothing. Not considered as a hand

Whichever version of poker you play, the hands in the table above are the ones you will be trying to make. In some games, such as Omaha Hi/Lo, Seven-Card Stud Hi/Lo, and Razz, there is another type of hand known as a low-hand in which players are trying to hit five cards below a nine. (We'll see more on this later.)

Poker Hand Values

Now that you know the poker hands, we'll show you their relative values.

Pairs

A pair is the most common hand in poker. High pairs – A-A, K-K, Q-Q and J-J – win many games; middle and low pairs usually lose.

In general, pairs are dangerous hands (for you) and they are often over-played by beginners. Many players place too much reliance on top pairs, thinking the game is as good as won, and persist with middle and low pairs in the hope of making a set (a three-of-a-kind). In the case of top pairs, they forget that these are still the lowest type of hand and are easily beaten.

Over-playing pairs is dangerous in low-limit Hold'em, where many players will draw to the river if there is a chance of making a straight or flush. The more players there are staying in the game to the end, the more likely it is that a pair will be beaten. As you move up the limits, however, where the stakes are higher, players are naturally more cautious with the result that pairs have more value.

Note that, statistically, a pair of aces will win approximately one game in three. A pair of twos, on the other hand, will win only one game in twelve.

Two Pairs

Many large pots are won with these hands, especially if one of the pairs is A-A or K-K. A two-pair hand can be particularly lethal if neither pair is on the board. (Such a pair is known as a split pair.) For example:

Flop Cards

Turn Card

River Card

...cont'd

Hot tip

A flush is a five card hand as it requires five cards of the same suit. Because you have only two start cards, a flush is only possible when there are three cards of the same suit on the table.

Hot tip

An inside straight is where the hand is completed by an inside card. For example: 4-5-7-8 needs a 6.
An outside straight needs an outside card. For example: T-J-Q-K is completed by a 9 or an A. Because two cards can complete the hand, the chances of completing an outside straight are twice as good.

A player holding A-A is going to love these community cards. There's no chance of being beaten by a flush (see top margin note), a straight is very unlikely, and there's a king, which, hopefully, another player has paired with and will bet on. There's no apparent danger to the aces.

However, an opponent has been dealt K-9 giving them two (split) pairs. The player holding A-A has no way of deducing this from the cards on the board. He has to assume that he has the best hand at this point and thus put in a large raise. Unless he is lucky enough to hit a third ace to give him a set (see below), he's going to lose a large pot here.

Playing a two-pair if one of the pairs is on the board requires more caution, as there is a chance that someone has a third card of that rank, making a set.

Sets (Three-of-a-Kind)

Also known as "trips", this is another hand that can catch players by surprise. If only one of the three cards is on the board (a concealed set), opponents have no indication that they are up against one.

Players holding sets will usually win the game as they beat the most common hands, pairs and two-pairs. However, you need to be aware of the possibility of another player holding a straight, or a flush. This is particularly likely at a ten-seat table.

Straights

If you get one of these you can be fairly confident that you are going to win the game. The only hand that's likely to beat you is a higher straight, or a flush.

These hands can be either low-ended or high-ended. For example, a low-ended straight would be when you hold 7-8 and the board (the community cards) is 9-10-J. If you hold K-Q with the same board then you have a high-end straight.

The problem with straights is that it's often fairly obvious from the board cards, and the way he/she is betting, when a player is holding one. Because of this, often a straight will only win a smallish pot as the other players can see the danger and thus fold.

Flushes

A flush is an excellent hand to hold and it is unlikely to be beaten. Because of this, many players will draw to the river if there is a chance of hitting one. However, in most cases this is a mistake. We'll look at this in more detail later on, but for now let's see what the statistics tell us.

Being dealt two suited cards is common – you can expect this once in every four hands.

If you have a three-to-a-flush (two more cards of the same suit needed) after the flop, the probability of hitting two more suits on the turn and the river is 1 in 23. Thus, the chances of completing your flush are slim, and a huge pot will be needed to justify playing the hand out (see Playing the Percentages on pages 40-43).

If you have a four-to-a-flush after the flop (one more card needed), the probability of making the flush on the turn or river is 1 in 2, which are much better odds. However, if the turn card doesn't complete the flush, the odds of making it on the river card go up to 1 in 4.

The most important statistic of all is that two suited start cards will make a flush once in every 16 attempts. This indicates quite clearly just what a futile exercise chasing after flushes really is. Furthermore, if you play low-suited cards, there is also the danger that even if you hit the flush, a higher one will beat you anyway.

Many players lose a lot of money by chasing after this hand (and straights). When they do finally get one, the pot is rarely large enough to cover the losses incurred on the previous attempts, never mind show a profit.

Hot tip

Throughout this book, you will see many references to straight and flush draws. This refers to a hand with which a player is hoping to make either a straight or a flush.

Don't forget

Remember this statistic: the odds of hitting a flush from two suited start cards is 1 in 16.

Beware

Whenever you get a full house where three of the cards are on the board and your pair is not too strong, be extremely wary if another player raises.

...cont'd

Full Houses

Upon hitting one of these most players can't get their money in the pot fast enough. However, you need to be aware that a full house can be made in two ways, and if it falls the wrong way you could actually have a terrible hand.

This is due to the fact that a full house is essentially two hands – a pair and a set. If the set is on the board then everybody else has it as well. So if two players are also holding a pair (which is quite common) then both will have a full house. It then becomes a game of pairs, and the player with the highest pair will win (and there's also the possibility that someone might have the fourth card of the set's rank to give them quads – see below).

For the player with the lower pair, this is a truly horrible hand to get as he/she will have put a load of money in the pot before waking up to the reality of the situation.

The thrill of hitting a full house often blinds a player to the possibility that another player might have a higher one, or quads. This is by no means an uncommon scenario.

Four-of-a-Kind (Quads)

Hitting four cards of the same rank is very unusual. The possibility that someone has higher quads is always there but, in reality, is so unlikely that you can discount it completely.

The only problem you will have is how to play the hand so as to extract the maximum amount of money from your opponents.

Straight Flushes

A straight flush is the ultimate poker hand, be it a royal flush or otherwise. Quite simply, if you get one of these, you are virtually unbeatable. The chances of getting one, though, are very remote.

As with quads, the only decision you will face is how to play the hand in order to get the most out of it.

Hand Elements

Two elements of a poker hand that are commonly overlooked by beginners are kickers and overcards. Understanding what these are, and their relevance in a game of poker, is essential.

Kickers

Kickers are the left-over cards after a hand is declared, and are the determining factor in who wins if two or more players have the same hand. Kickers are only relevant in hands that don't require five cards, i.e. sets, two-pairs, one-pair, and high card situations. Here is an example:

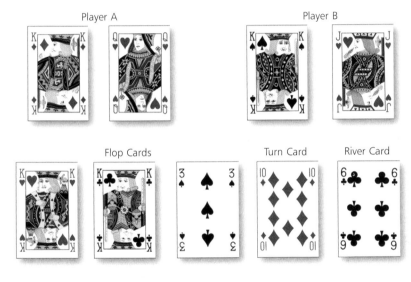

Here, both players have a set (three kings). However, Player A has a queen kicker while Player B has a jack kicker. Thus, Player A takes the pot.

Kickers are particularly relevant in situations where you are attempting to win the game with a pair. At a ten-seat table, it is not unusual for two players to be holding the same pair, usually the higher ones, such as kings, queens and jacks. The higher the kicker, the higher the chance of the pair winning.

...cont'd

Overcards

An overcard can be defined in two ways:

1)   It is a start card that is higher than any card on the board. For example, if you hold A-K and the board is Q-8-5, you have two overcards, as shown below.

Start Cards   Flop Cards

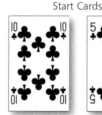

2)   It is a card on the board that is higher than either of your start cards. For example, if you hold T-5 and the board is 2-4-A, there is an overcard (the ace) on the board, as shown below.

Start Cards   Flop Cards

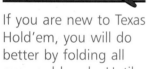

There will be many occasions when all you hold on the flop are two overcards, as shown in example 1 above. If the best hand you are likely to make is no more than a pair then as a general rule, you should fold.

However, if the hand offers two or more possibilities, such as a high pair, plus a straight or flush, then it will be worth continuing with it. In this situation, the decision is usually determined by the pot odds.

Drawing Hands

A drawing hand is one that needs to be improved. For example, 5-6 is a drawing hand because the chances of winning with a 6 high are remote. A pair of kings, on the other hand, is a made hand and will win many pots with no improvement.

The three most common drawing hands players try to make are sets, straights, and flushes. When they do hit them, they will usually win the pot. However, you need to be aware of two things here:

First, for every time you hit the hand, there will be many more when you don't (and almost always lose money). This takes us on to the second point.

Second, when you do hit the hand, the pot must be big enough to cover the odds against hitting it.

The majority of hands are drawing hands, so playing them all is a sure-fire way to lose your bankroll. To win with these hands, there are three factors you must consider:

- Which hands to play
- Is the pot large enough to make the play worthwhile
- At what point to give up on the hand

Something else to remember is that straights and flushes require at least three of the hand's cards to be on the board. This often makes it fairly obvious to your opponents what they might be facing. For example, if three cards of a straight are on the board, e.g. 5-6-7, and the turn card is an 8, this is going to kill the game – anyone who doesn't hold a 4 or a 9 will fold immediately if an opponent bets.

For this reason, pots won with these hands are often quite small. To win a large pot usually requires the hand to be completed on the turn or river, by which stage money has already gone into the pot.

We'll take a closer look at this in Chapter 5.

Beware

Over-playing drawing hands will result in a slow, but steady, erosion of your bankroll.

Don't forget

The whole purpose of playing poker is to win money. If it's costing you $10 to win $8 then you are losing money. If you are playing a drawing hand, you must be sure that, if you win with it, the size of the pot warrants the risk.

Table Position

A player's position at the table in relation to the dealer is an extremely important strategic factor in Texas Hold'em, and one that is totally ignored by many players. Table position is a major factor when deciding which start cards should be played and which should be folded.

Early Position

At a ten-seat table, the four players sitting to the left of the dealer are in early positions. Because they have to act first in the betting, they are at a disadvantage as they cannot observe how their opponents will act before making their move.

For example, in an early position you might bet on a marginal hand and then find yourself faced with a raise by a later player. If you'd been in a late position, however, the raise would have come before it was your turn to act, and so instead of betting on the marginal hand, you could have folded and saved yourself some chips.

This is why it's so important to play only the top start cards in early position. If another player does raise you, it doesn't matter because you're going to play these cards anyway. In fact, you don't mind being raised because at this point in the game you will usually have the best hand.

Middle Position

The three players to the left of the early position players are said to be in a middle position.

Pre-flop, these players don't have the benefits of late position, but neither do they have the disadvantage of being in an early position. Because they are between the two, they are able to play a few more hands than they would in an early position, but not as many as they could in a late position.

After the flop, they have the benefit of having seen half their opponents act, but are handicapped by the fact that they don't know what the other half are going to do.

Don't forget

A very important thing to remember about table position is that you will be in the same position for every betting round in any one hand. (The only exception to this is the blind players who are last to act in the first betting round, but first to act in every subsequent round.)

Late Position

The final three players are in late position. This is the best position on the table as it provides many advantages, the most important of which is that they have a lot of information available to them. Being one of the last to act gives you two crucial pieces of data:

1) how many opponents you have, and 2) their actions.

Let's assume you have Td-5d. This is a drawing hand and with these particular cards, you will be hoping to hit a flush. The problem with drawing hands is that the odds against completing them are high. This means you need to win a large pot to make the play profitable, and the only way the pot will be large is if enough of your opponents are betting.

Being the last to act, you will know exactly how many players have made a bet. If seven players fold and only two bet, you would fold your Td-5d. But if seven bet and only two fold then you could play the hand. In an early position, you would have folded immediately as you wouldn't have had the opportunity to see how many players made a bet.

A low pair is another example of a hand that should only be played in a late position, and with this you would be looking to hit a set. However, you wouldn't want to put too much money on these cards, and would only play them if you could see the flop cheaply. Being last to act tells you this as well: if no one has raised, you can see the flop for one bet, which makes the play worthwhile. If someone has raised, however, you will have to pay two bets; also, their raise indicates they have a good hand. So you would fold.

Other advantages include:

- Being able to buy a free card (see page 45)
- The opportunity to "steal" the blind money
- Opportunities to bluff (see pages 47-48)
- Being able to "buy" a better table position (see page 45)

Don't forget

Late position allows a player to take a chance with lesser hands that would be folded in an earlier position for fear of a subsequent raise.

Playing Styles

While using the right strategy and playing the percentages will give you a big edge over the majority of players, there are other ways to increase your edge over them further. One of these is being able to recognize the different playing styles adopted by players, most of which result in consistent losses. Once you can do this and understand why they lose, you will then have a good idea of what they are thinking and be able to second-guess them.

Loose-Aggressive

Loose-aggressive players are known as maniacs as they play most hands and love to raise (often with mediocre hands). They have no grasp of strategy, no conception of the percentages, and go all-in at the drop of a hat. They rely totally on luck and bluffs and, in the short term, can be successful. When their luck goes though, so do their chips.

Loose-Passive

Slightly better than the maniac, the loose-passive player also plays most hands. However, players of this kind rarely raise; instead, they simply call or check most bets. As they're never in control of the betting and don't take advantage of good hands by raising, they are destined to be losers – not as quickly as the maniac, but losers nevertheless.

Tight-Passive

Known as "rocks", these players take no risks at all. They fold continuously, playing only with the very top hands. However, when they get that elusive top hand, they don't play it aggressively enough. Instead of raising and re-raising, they will often just call and check. The problem with this type of play is that it is very predictable. On the rare occasions these players do raise, everyone knows they have a very good hand and folds immediately. They win only small pots usually.

Tight-Aggressive

If there is an ideal playing style, this is it. These players play only good start cards but play them aggressively by raising at every opportunity. Bad hands, they fold.

Tells

A poker tell is any habit or physical reaction that gives other players information about your hand. For example, some people when holding a really strong set of cards are unable to hide a slight tremor in their hands. Others will glance at them repeatedly as if to reassure themselves that their eyes are not deceiving them. There are many more, and experienced players know them all and act on them.

However, in online poker your opponents are invisible, so is it possible to get any tells? To a lesser degree, yes. The following are often a good indication regarding the strength of your opponents' hands.

A Long Delay Followed by a Bet or Raise
Many players who take longer than usual before betting are trying to create the impression that they have a weak hand and are having to think hard about whether it's worth playing, when in reality they actually have a strong hand. They do this to encourage you to bet.

Checking
Players usually check when they have a weak hand as it enables them to stay in the game at no cost.

Instantaneous Bet or Raise on the Turn or River
This is a sign of confidence and usually indicates a very strong hand. Players who do this (especially when raising) are confident that they have the best hand and can't wait to take your money. If someone does this to you, be careful; take a few seconds to re-evaluate the board and see if there's something you've missed.

Check-Raise
A check-raise is when a player initially checks, and then when the betting comes round again, raises. The check is to make the other players think he or she has a weak hand and thus put money in the pot. This accomplished, the player then starts raising. When you see someone doing this, it is a sure sign that they have a good hand.

Beware

In the latter stages of a hand be careful if a player bets instantaneously. This usually means he/she has a very good hand and is confident of winning with it.

Inside the Mind of a Pro

We're going to try to get inside the head of a top poker player and identify the characteristics that make him so good. Comparing yourself to this hypothetical character will give you a good idea whether or not you have what it takes to play winning poker.

Purpose

Our man has one thing in mind when he sits down at a poker table: taking the other players' money. He's not there to enjoy himself or to pass the time – this isn't a game to him; it's business.

Focus

He allows nothing to distract him from his purpose. He can't be bullied or intimidated by the other players. When he's playing, he shuts his private life away – personal problems do not affect his play.

Intelligence

He has an analytical brain and is able to do quick mental calculations that enable him to figure out the percentages. He knows which hands to play and how far to play them. He can "work out" his opponents and second-guess them.

Discipline

Our man is able to "shut up shop" when things are going against him. There is no way this guy is going to lose a cent more than he has to. This enables him to ride out losing streaks that would bust lesser players.

Observation

He sees everything. He looks for tables with weak players, he knows all the poker tells, and he recognizes danger signs. He can often tell you what cards you are holding.

Patience

He doesn't expect to be winning all the time; he knows it isn't possible. He'll just sit and wait for good opportunities.

4 Poker Ploys

Basic strategy will only take you so far. The techniques described here will take your game to a higher level; one that few of your opponents will be able to match.

40 Playing the Percentages

41 Pot Odds

41 Hand Odds

44 Raising

46 Check-Raising

46 Slow-Playing

47 Bluffing

49 Deception

Playing the Percentages

Far too many poker players base their game on luck. They play speculative hands *hoping* to catch the card they need, they play so-called "lucky cards" because they've won with them before, and they attribute their losses to bad luck. Periodically, they do get lucky, but the law of averages says that for every lucky streak they get, they will also have an unlucky one.

Luck is a factor in poker, of course (as it is in any game of chance), but to a good player, it is much less of one; it is a short term issue, and in the long term it's largely irrelevant. The reason for this is that good players are able to recognize when the odds are in their favor and when they aren't. This knowledge enables them to drop hands that in the long term are going to lose them money. Inexperienced players who don't understand odds will bet on these hands.

As a very simple illustration, consider this: Diamond Jack says to Bill "Let's toss a coin 1000 times. If it comes down heads, you pay me $100 and if it comes down tails, I'll pay you $90". If Bill accepts, he'll win $90 500 times and lose $100 500 times. At the end of the 1000 spins, he'll be $5000 out of pocket. Bill may get lucky periodically and he may find himself up at times, but over 1000 spins the law of averages will take over. This is an impossible game for Bill to win – the odds are stacked against him.

Fortunately, Bill's not that stupid. There's no way he's going to bet on a game he simply cannot win. He just laughs at the ludicrous suggestion.

"OK then" says Diamond Jack (who's an experienced poker player), "I can see you're not going to fall for that one. How about 1000 hands of poker?" Bill (who's not an experienced poker player) foolishly agrees, and after 1000 hands, he's $5000 down. He had no more chance in the poker game than he would have had spinning the coin. While he understands the concept of odds, he had no idea of its importance in a game of poker. Diamond Jack did.

Hot tip

If you are a percentage player, you are not a gambler. You will be doing exactly the same thing that casinos do: stacking the odds in your favor. If you get it right, it will be impossible for you to lose in the long term.
    Compare this with the player who doesn't play the percentages: that player is a gambler, and in the long term will find it impossible not to lose.

Diamond Jack knows that he's going to lose more hands than he wins – with anything up to ten opponents, it can be no other way. So the only way he can make a consistent profit is to win more with the hands that do win than he loses on the hands that don't. The odds must be stacked in his favor, as they would have been in the coin toss scenario. With really good hands this is not so important as he will win with most of these anyway. It's the lesser hands where he has a good chance of losing where it really applies.

To know what odds he is facing on a hand, he needs to consider two factors: the pot odds and the hand odds.

Pot Odds

Pot odds is the relationship between the size of the pot and the size of a bet. For example: if there is $10 in the pot and you have to call a $2 bet to stay in the game, then the pot odds are 5:1. The higher the pot odds, the more value you are getting for your bet.

Hand Odds

This is the statistical likelihood of making a particular hand. To work it out simply divide the number of cards that won't complete the hand by the number of cards that will (the latter are known as "outs"). For example: your pocket cards are J-T and the flop is Q-3-9. You need an 8 or a K to complete a straight. What are the chances of making it?

Of the 47 unseen cards (52 cards in the pack minus the two start cards and the three flop cards) there are eight cards that will complete the hand (four kings and four eights) and 39 that won't. Simply divide 39 by eight to give a figure of 4.8. Thus, approximately every five times you play this hand, you will complete the straight once; the other four times, you won't.

Using the Percentages

Simply compare the hand odds to the pot odds. If the odds against making your hand are higher than the pot odds, then the potential payoff from winning doesn't justify the bet.

Hot tip

A quick method of working out approximate hand odds in percentages is as follows:

At the flop: multiply the number of outs by four. For example, if you have a flush draw, there are nine outs: 9 x 4 = 36. So you have roughly a 36% chance of completing the flush (the exact odds are actually 35%).

At the turn or river: multiply the outs by two. Using our flush example: 9 x 2 = 18. You have roughly an 18% chance (the exact odds are 19.6%).

...cont'd

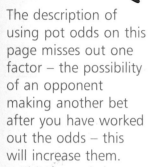

Hot tip

The description of using pot odds on this page misses out one factor – the possibility of an opponent making another bet after you have worked out the odds – this will increase them.

This factor is known as "implied odds". Because of it, you can sometimes bet on a hand that the pot odds say you shouldn't because the implied odds make it correct to do so.

For example: the pot holds $200 and the bet to you is $20. Thus, the pot odds are 10:1. If the odds of hitting your hand are 1:11, you should fold. But if two opponents each make another bet, the pot goes up to $240 and the pot odds become 12:1. If you have reason to believe they will both make the bet, the implied odds say you will be correct to call.

For example: you are holding 5-6, and the flop shows an 8-9-A. You need a 7 to complete an inside straight. There are four outs for your hand (four 7s in the deck). The odds of making this hand are 1:11. There is $80 in the pot, and it's $10 to call; this makes the pot odds 8:1. Thus, for the hand to break even it must win once in eight instances. However, the hand odds say it will win once in eleven instances. If you bet on this hand eleven times, you will have staked a total of $110 and won $80 – a net loss of $30.

Another example: your start cards are both spades and the flop brings two more – you need one more spade to make a flush. As there are thirteen spades in the pack and four are already showing, you have nine outs. The odds of making a hand with nine outs are 1:4. Assuming the betting and the size of the pot are the same as in the example above, the pot odds are 8:1. Again, you need the hand to win once in eight instances to break even. The hand odds say the hand will win once in four instances, so if you bet on it four times, you will have staked $40 and won $80 – a net profit of $40.

All this is dependent on the hand actually winning when you hit it and, of course, sometimes it won't. To cover this possibility, you need some leeway in the pot odds (they need to be slightly higher). If the odds are good, the leeway's probably there already, but if not, the hand may be too risky to play.

All serious poker players play the percentages and it gives them a definite edge over the players who don't. To do it, though, (particularly online where the pace is fast), requires some quick mental arithmetic that is not so easy to perform in the heat of a game. If you are playing online, however, there is nothing to prevent you from using some aids.

Working out the pot odds is easy with a calculator; it takes only a couple of seconds. As regards hand odds, all you need is the following table, which shows you the odds against making the most common hands in Texas Hold'em.

...cont'd

The Hand column shows common hands, and the Outs column shows the number of outs (cards) that can complete the hand. Taking the first line as an example, if you have a set after the flop, there is only one card, or out, that can give you a four-of-a-kind.

The Turn column gives the odds of completing the hand at the turn, and the River column gives the odds of completing the hand at the river.

Outs	Hand	Turn	River
1	Set to four-of-a-kind Inside straight flush draw to straight flush	1:46	1:23
2	One pair to a set Open-ended straight flush draw to straight flush	1:23	1:12
3	High card to a pair	1:15	1:8
4	Two pairs to a full house Inside straight draw to a straight	1:11	1:6
5	Pair to two-pair or a set	1:9	1:5
6	Two high cards to a pair	1:7	1:4
7	Set to a full house or four-of-a-kind	1:6	1:3
8	Open-ended straight draw to a straight	1:5	1:3
9	Flush draw to a flush	1:4	1:2
10	Over-pair with an outside straight draw to a set, or a straight	1:4	1:2
11	Overcard with an outside straight draw to a pair, or a straight	1:4	1:2
12	Flush and inside straight draw, to a flush or a straight	1:3.8	1:2.2
13	One pair and an outside straight draw, to two pairs or better	1:3.5	1:2
14	Outside straight draw and two overcards, to a straight or a pair	1:3.2	1:1.9
15	Outside straight flush draw to a straight flush, flush or straight	1:3	1:1.8

Hot tip

Committing the odds in the table opposite to memory, so that they can be recalled instantly, will prove to be very beneficial. If you don't fancy the idea of doing this, though, at least memorize the odds for flush and straight draws. You'll be using these all the time.

43

Raising

Until players understand the power of the raise and the various ways it can help them achieve their goal, i.e. win the pot, they're never going to succeed at poker.

Building the Pot
This is the most obvious reason to raise. You're sitting on A-A and the flop is A-A-K. You've hit a monster hand and want to win as much with it as possible. So the natural inclination in this situation is to raise. While this might work, it may, however, have the opposite effect. It could actually intimidate your opponents into folding and result in you completely wasting the hand.

The trick with using the raise to build the pot, therefore, is picking the right time to do it. Using the above example, if you raise on the flop, players who haven't made a hand will almost certainly fold. However, if you call, or maybe even just check, they may stay in for the turn card, which, hopefully, will complete their hand giving them an incentive to bet. Now will be the time to raise. If there are several players still in, you might even leave it until the river before you raise. Remember, the more cards your opponents see, the better the chance they have of making a hand.

Limiting the Competition
Many players fail to grasp one of the most fundamental concepts in poker – the more opponents you have, the less your chances are of winning. Therefore, in most situations, you want as few players in the hand as possible. A typical example of this is a pair: J-J, for instance. Play this to the end against nine opponents and it's extremely unlikely to win. If there are only two opponents, though, it stands a much better chance.

So what you do is raise pre-flop. By doing so, you are telling the opposition that you have a good hand and that they'd be advised to fold. Hopefully, they will take the hint and do so. While not all will, especially in a low-limit game where players tend to take more risks, enough will do so to give the hand a much better chance of taking the pot.

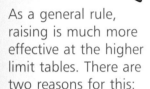

Hot tip

As a general rule, raising is much more effective at the higher limit tables. There are two reasons for this:

First, the monetary value of the bet will be much higher, which means that a player who calls it will be risking more.

Second, players at the higher limits are more aware of poker strategy, and thus will be more likely to respect a raise.

Gaining Information

The raise provides a way of finding out the strength of an opponent's hand (albeit at a price). For example: your pocket cards are 9-T and the flop is K-3-T, giving you T-T. There are two players still in, and either could be sitting there with K-K. A raise at this point is likely to achieve one of two things: first, both opponents might fold, thus presenting you with an uncontested pot or, second, one might re-raise you. With one king already showing, the re-raise tells you quite clearly that he or she probably has two kings, so you fold. OK, it's cost you a bet to find out you're beaten, but it may well have saved you several bets down the line.

Buying a Free Card

The purpose here is to get to see the next but one community card without having to pay a full bet. Typically, this is done at the flop when the betting is still at the lower limit. For this ploy to work, you need to be in a late position and facing limited opposition.

For example: your pocket cards are 9s-8s and the flop is Kd-Qs-6h. This is not a great hand; at the moment you are probably beaten by K-K or Q-Q. It does have limited drawing potential, though – a backdoor flush or straight. Both are long shots and, unless the pot is huge, you would probably fold it. However, if you are the last to act, throwing in a raise might get you a free card on the river. How? By raising, you will probably make your opponents check on the turn card. If they do then you will have the option to check as well and will be able to see the river card for "free".

Buying Position

You're to the right of the three late position players. You've got a hand that you would play from late position but are wary of playing in your present middle position. If the late position opponents are tight players, raising could well make them all fold. If they do, you've just bought late position, a position you'll hold for every subsequent betting round.

Check-Raising

Check-raising is when you check on a betting round and then when the betting comes back round to you, you raise. There are two reasons to make this play:

1) When you have a nut hand and want to deceive the opposition into thinking you actually have a weak hand – hence the check. Hopefully, one or more of them will make a bet thus putting money into the pot. This accomplished, you can now raise. If you had raised straight away, they may all have folded

2) As a bluff. Good opponents realize that a check-raise usually means a good hand and if they don't have anything much themselves, will usually fold. However, this will only work against good players; bad players will see no significance in the play and may well call the bet

This is another way of taking down small pots with nothing.

Slow-Playing

A hand is usually slow-played when it can't be beaten, or is very unlikely to be, with the intention of keeping as many players in the game as possible. This is to give them every opportunity to hit their hand; hopefully, a good one that will encourage them to put money in the pot.

To do this, you check or call, rather than raising, so as not to scare anyone off. It's only on the turn, or even the river, that you make your move by raising (this is when the bets double). By this time, any player who's going to make a good hand will have done so.

However, your hand must be unbeatable to slow-play it. This is because by doing so, you are giving opponents the opportunity to see more cards cheaply. If your hand is vulnerable, there is always a danger they will end up hitting a better one.

Beware

Check-raising and slow-playing should only be done when you are certain your hand cannot be beaten. Remember, by checking you are giving opponents the opportunity of seeing the next card for free.

Bluffing

Bluffing is an important element of poker strategy, and against the right kind of opponent, and in the right type of game, it can be extremely effective. However, in very loose games, such as those commonly found at the low- and micro-limit tables, it is much less so.

First, loose players tend to bite at anything as by their very nature they cannot be intimidated. At the higher-limit tables, however, where players are more circumspect, a bluff is far more likely to be respected. Second, if a player doesn't need to put much in the pot to call a bet, as is the case in fixed-limit games, a bluff loses much of its power. In a no-limit game, though, where bets can be huge, it is a powerful weapon.

So when is it appropriate to try a bluff? The following are some typical situations:

When Your Opponents are Tight Players
Tight players are careful players – they don't like taking risks. There are two situations where they can often be bluffed. The first is at the pre-flop stage. Note that for this to be effective, you need to be in late position (last to act, ideally). With a table full of tight players, it is not uncommon for most of them to fold or check, and just one or two to bet. Throwing in a raise from last position will often make these players fold.

The second is after the flop. A tight player who's missed the flop will either fold or, if the chance arises, check, in the hope of getting a free card. If you are in late position and two or three opponents all check to you, by raising you are forcing them to call a double bet to stay in the game, and often they will fold – giving you an uncontested pot.

On the River
Often, players paying to see the river card will be on a drawing hand and will have failed to make it. In this situation, most players will usually check if the option is available.

Hot tip

When considering a bluff, it is very important that you pick the right type of opponent. Generally, these should be tight or timid players. Also, don't try and bluff more than two; it rarely works.

Beware

At fixed-limit tables, bluffing is usually a pointless exercise that is more likely to lose money than it is to win it. You simply cannot make a big enough bet for it to carry any weight.

Hot tip

As a general rule, you should only bluff when you have some sort of a hand in case your bluff is called. This will give you a chance; if you have nothing at all, you will have to concede the hand.

Beware

Be careful not to overdo it. Bluffing is most effective when it is done sparingly. Do it too often and your opponents will soon cotton on.

...cont'd

As anyone with a good hand is going to be betting on the final round, rather than checking, this is a good time to try a bluff.

Representing a Hand

With this play you are trying to convince the opposition that you have a specific hand, such as a straight, flush or trips. Say the board cards are 6-K-4-T-6. You have two opponents and they both check to you on the river. By putting in a raise, you are indicating that you probably have a 6 in your hand and thus have trips. If neither of them have a better hand, they will probably fold. The same applies to a flush or straight draw – bet as though you have it and very often the opposition will fold.

This is a useful way of picking up small pots.

When Not to Bluff

Almost as important as knowing when to bluff, is knowing when not to. As a general rule, don't try and bluff several opponents. Pre-flop, when they don't have any money in the pot, this may work as they aren't losing anything by folding. After the flop though, it's a different matter.

As soon as you get caught bluffing, the other players will label you as a bluffer, and will be more inclined to call your bets in future. Wait a while before trying it again to give them time to forget about it.

Never bluff against bad players – it rarely works. Bad players are likely to call anything and everything, a fact that renders a bluff against them utterly pointless. Also, don't bluff if you are in an early table position. You need to see your opponents' actions first.

The opponent is probably the most important factor. Aggressive players who hate to "yield", and maniacs who can't resist betting, should not be bluffed. Weak, timid players, on the other hand, can be.

Deception

The ability to deceive opponents is a very important factor in poker. If you can persuade them that you have a much poorer hand than is actually the case, you are going to take money from them – slow-playing is an example of how you do this. Sometimes, you want to do the opposite and make them think you have a much better hand than theirs; this is bluffing.

If you never try to deceive the opposition then you become a predictable player – one who is going to find it difficult to win. You must be able to mix up your play on occasion, so that your opponents are never quite sure of what you're up to. We've mentioned ways to do this above; here are some others:

Deliberately Play Bad Hands
On page 52, you will see that you should play only certain hands pre-flop. However, if you stick to this religiously, it won't be long before your opponents put you down as a very tight player who must be respected whenever you raise the pot. While you will still win pots, generally they are going to be small ones as opponents aren't going to take any risks with you. Hands that they would play against a loose player, they will fold. When you turn up A-A, raise, and then the entire table folds, you are going to be extremely exasperated.

So now and again, do the opposite. Wait until you've got a really bad hand, say 6-2, and the flop is completely against you – K-J-T, for example; only an idiot would bet in this situation. Take this right to the showdown so that the other players will see what you have been playing with. This play will stick in their minds far longer than your good plays. While you will lose money when you do this, the pay-off will come when you get a good hand and your opponents call your bets because they think you may be doing the same thing again.

Switch Gears
Generally, players adopt one of four playing styles (see page 36) and, often, they aren't even aware of it.

Hot tip

Poker is as much about playing the opposition as it is about playing the cards. You should always be watching what your opponents do. Also, don't forget that they will be watching you, so give them something to think about by doing different things occasionally.

...cont'd

If you follow the advice in this book, you will be a tight-aggressive player, usually playing only the top hands but playing them aggressively. While this is undoubtedly the best way to play poker, if you *always* play this way, you become predictable.

Don't forget

Even if you lose some chips when playing loosely, you will win them back (and more) with your good hands. Opponents will be much more inclined to call your bets when they think you play bad hands.

This is the last thing you want, so, suddenly, become a loose player. Pick the right time to do this, though. Remember, loose players lose, and losing isn't in your game plan.

The ideal time to do it is when the cards are falling in your favor. When you're on a hot streak, you can play virtually anything – even rubbishy hands like 7-2 can turn into sets and full houses. As soon as your hot streak ends, change back to your normal style.

By doing this occasionally, there will always be an element of doubt in your opponents' minds. As a result, they are much more likely to make the wrong calls against you.

Tells

We saw on page 37 how it is possible for online players to give definite clues regarding the strength of their hands by the speed with which they make their moves.

Most online players are aware of this, which gives you another way of being deceptive (assuming you are playing online). For example, say you have an ace high flush on the river. In this situation many players will bet instantaneously knowing they can't lose – you will see this all the time. If you do the same thing yourself, it may well make an opponent pause for thought. So instead, let ten seconds or so go by before making your bet.

However, don't make the mistake of over-doing this by waiting until your time to act is almost up. This is another classic indication of a player holding a very good hand. Save this move for when you have missed your hand and want to try and bluff your opponent out of the pot. Combining this with a raise will often do the trick.

5 Fixed-Limit Texas Hold'em Strategy

By now you will know how to play Texas Hold'em, know how to increase your chances of winning by good table selection, and be aware of techniques such as check–raising and pot odds. In this chapter, we show you how to put all these factors together in a strategy that will enable you to beat most players, or at the very least, as a beginner, prevent you from losing while you gain experience.

52 Start Cards

53 Pre-Flop Play

57 Playing From the Blinds

59 Common Pre-Flop Mistakes

60 Playing the Flop

62 Playing Pairs on the Flop

64 Two Pairs on the Flop

66 Playing Sets on the Flop

68 Flush Draws on the Flop

70 Straight Draws on the Flop

72 Drawing Hands/Pot Odds

73 Playing a Flush or Straight on the Flop

74 Overcards on the Flop

75 Full House on the Flop

76 Playing the Turn

77 Playing the River

78 Short-Hand Play

79 Texas Hold'em Odds

Start Cards

Hot tip

The importance of start card selection cannot be overstated. As a general rule, you should be playing no more than one in five hands. If you are playing more than this, you are playing cards that you shouldn't be.

An essential part of mastering Texas Hold'em is knowing which start cards are playable and which are not. The player's position at the table is also a determining factor here.

The table below shows exactly which hands can be played; any hands not in the table should be folded immediately:

Playable Starting Hands
Top Hands
A-A, K-K, Q-Q, J-J, A-Ks, A-Ko
Good Hands
T-T, 9-9, A-Qs, A-Js, A-Ts, K-Qs, K-Js, Q-Js, J-Ts, A-Qo, K-Qo
Average Hands
8-8, 7-7, K-Ts, Q-Ts, Q-9s, J-9s, T-9s, T-8s, 9-8s, 9-7s, 8-7s, 7-6s, 6-5s, A-Jo, K-Jo, Q-Jo, J-To, A-xs
Marginal Hands
6-6, 5-5, 4-4, 3-3, 2-2, 5-4s, 4-3s, K-9s, Q-8s, J-8s, T-7s, 8-6s, 7-5s, 6-4s, 5-3s, K-xs, A-To, K-To, Q-To, J-9o, T-9o, 9-8o
A – Ace, K – King, Q – Queen, J – Jack, T – Ten, 2-9 – card value, x – unknown card, s – same suit, o – different suits

The hand recommendations are based on a typical middle-limit ten-player game where the action is neither tight nor loose. By playing only these cards, the majority of the time you will have an edge over most of your opponents as you will be playing only the best hands.

Another advantage of this basic strategy is that, to a certain degree, you will be immunized against losing streaks and the mind games these can play with you. If you are only playing a few hands (with this strategy, you will be folding approximately 80% of the time), your losses in a bad streak will be much less.

One negative aspect of playing in this way is boredom. Folding hand after hand can become very tedious after a while. However, watching your bankroll steadily slip away is not very exciting either, and if you don't play this way, that's just what may happen.

Pre-Flop Play

Now we'll take a closer look at these hands, explaining in detail how you should play them and why.

Early Positions

These are the four seats to the immediate left of the dealer. Early position players are at a disadvantage as they have to act first, and for this reason they must be very careful in their hand selection.

Playing the Top Hands

With any of these, you raise. If you are re-raised, raise again. Don't hold back: it is essential that you play these hands aggressively. There are two reasons for doing this:

1) To get money in the pot. If two or three players call your raise, money is going into the pot. Remember, at this stage you probably have the best hand

2) To make as many of your opponents as possible fold, thus denying them the chance to draw a better hand on and after the flop. Your hand may rule the roost pre-flop, but afterwards, it might well not do so. The more players who see the flop, the higher the chances of one of them hitting a better hand

Now you may well be thinking that if you make all your opponents fold, there's going to be nothing in the pot worth winning, and an excellent hand will have been wasted. However, at a ten-seat table it's very unlikely that everybody will fold. One or two players will call your raise, which is exactly what you want. Money will go in the pot and, against limited opposition, your top hand has a very good chance of taking it without any improvement. If they do all fold, you still get the blinds money.

What you must not do is slow-play these hands. Checking and calling will result in several of your opponents staying in, and all too often at least one of them will end up hitting a better hand.

53

Hot tip

When you get a top starting hand, you must raise to thin out the opposition. Remember, pairs (even big ones) do not fare well against many opponents.

Hot tip

At a ten-seat table, usually four or five players will fold immediately. That leaves you with three or four opponents. If they all bet, three or four bets will go into the pot.

However, if you raise and only two of them call, the same amount of money goes into the pot, but you have fewer players to beat.

...cont'd

Playing Good Hands

With these cards, you call and wait to see what your opponents do. If someone raises, as a general rule you should then fold. However, before you do, you need to consider the player making the raise (this is where opponent observation pays off). If it is a tight player who plays only top hands, then you should definitely fold. On the other hand, if it is a loose player who rarely folds, then call the bet. If the other player raises you again though, folding is probably the best thing to do (see top margin note).

Playing Average and Marginal Hands

In early position, these hands will only get you into trouble – fold and save your money for a better opportunity.

Middle Positions

Middle positions are the three seats to the left of the early position seats. This is half-way house – you have an idea of the table situation but not the complete picture.

Playing Top Hands

You play these in exactly the same way as you would in early position – raise and re-raise. Top hands don't fall very often – you must make the most of them when they do.

Playing Good Hands

How you play these is dependent on whether you are facing a raise. If not then you can raise with any of these hands. However, if there is a raise after you have played, you should call when the betting gets back to you. If two players raise, it's very likely that one of them has you beaten. Do not get into a raising war – just fold.

Playing Average Hands

These hands include many medium ranked connectors. This makes them ideal drawing hands with which to make a flush or a straight. Indeed, hitting one of these is the only way you are likely to win with this type of hand. Their face values are not high, so even if you make a pair, it's unlikely to be the highest pair.

Beware

A single raise from a loose player often means nothing. A re-raise, however, indicates that the player may actually have caught a good hand. Unless you also have one, play it safe by folding. Remember, there is no shortage of hands to play. When in doubt, the best policy is usually to leave it.

Hot tip

A connector is two cards of successive rank, e.g. 7-8 or K-Q. If the cards are of the same suit, they are a suited connector. Unless they are of a high face value, in which case they can also make a high pair, their value is limited to making a straight or a flush.

However, the odds against making a flush or straight are high. While you may be very lucky and get the three cards you need on the flop, it's much more likely that you will need the turn card, and probably the river card as well. As the bets double on these rounds, playing these hands can prove to be expensive.

Thus, to make the play worthwhile, there needs to be a lot of money in the pot. A large pot will usually require four or five players to be contributing, and this is the criterion you use when deciding whether to play a drawing hand. If only one or two opponents contribute to the pot pre-flop then the pot is usually not going to be large enough. In this case, fold.

Marginal Hands

These are mostly low pairs and gapped connectors. Few of them offer a realistic chance of making a good hand. If you bet on these cards from middle position, you run the risk of being raised by a late position player, in which case you would have to fold. The best thing to do with these hands is to dump them straight away.

Late Positions

Defined as the last three places at the table, late position gives you many advantages. You've seen your opponents' moves, and thus have a much better idea of which hands are playable and which aren't. Your decisions are easier to make and you have more options regarding the hands you can play.

Playing Top Hands

Raise, raise, raise – there's nothing more to say.

Playing Good Hands

You should play the good hands in exactly the same way as you would in middle position. If someone has already raised, just call the bet. Otherwise, raise and see what the others do. More than likely, most of them will fold. If the remaining players call, throw in another raise to try and narrow the field even more.

Hot tip

You might think that there's as much chance of making a straight with 3-5 as there is with 3-4. There's not. The bigger the gap between the cards, the less chance there is of making the straight.

Hot tip

About the only time you might consider just calling with a top hand is when you are holding Q-Q or J-J, and a very tight player has raised. Players of this type will usually only raise with A-A or K-K. Remember, play the player as well as the cards.

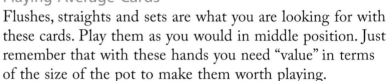

...cont'd

Remember, you're not playing top cards now; these hands are vulnerable. The fewer opponents you have, the better your chance of winning.

If someone re-raises you then just call. You definitely want to see the flop with these cards but you don't want to pay too high a price.

Playing Average Cards

Flushes, straights and sets are what you are looking for with these cards. Play them as you would in middle position. Just remember that with these hands you need "value" in terms of the size of the pot to make them worth playing.

If someone raises, you should generally fold. These hands are speculative, so you need to see the flop as cheaply as possible. However, if the pot looks like being a big one, it may be worth calling to see what the flop brings.

Playing Marginal Cards

One of the big advantages of being in a late position is that it allows you to play marginal hands that in any other position you would dump.

Again, the goal with these is flushes, straights and sets. Low- to middle-card straights can be a particularly effective hand to hold as most players will fold low-card hands. Therefore, the chances of someone else having one are slim. If the flop brings an ace or a king, giving someone a top pair, then a low or middle straight will clean up.

Remember though, these hands are speculative ones and should be played only if you can see the flop without too much expense.

Playing From the Blinds

For the majority of players, playing from the blind positions represents a small but steady drain on their bankroll. There are several reasons for this:

- They are playing "blind". A bet has to be made regardless of the strength of their hand

- They are the first to act in all betting rounds (with the exception of the first one)

- The good players are aware of the disadvantages faced by the blinds players and target them in an attempt to "steal" the blind money

Virtually everything is stacked against them. Let's see how you should deal with this situation.

Defending the Blinds

One of the main things the blinds have to contend with is opponents who attempt to steal the blind money. Typically, this will be a late position player who throws in a raise after everyone else has acted, hoping that they will all fold as a result. This player is targeting the blinds money, and assuming that the blinds players have the sense to fold anything other than a top hand.

The problem this causes is that if they do fold, the player will try it again – and again – and again. Other players will notice this and, before long, they'll be at it as well. If you allow this situation to develop, your stack will suffer (as will your table image), so something has to be done to stop it.

The solution is to nip it in the bud straight away. The first time someone tries this with you, re-raise them immediately, regardless of what cards you are holding. More than likely, they'll back down and fold. If they do bet, call. Whatever you do, don't fold. Even if you end up losing the hand, you'll have earned their respect and they'll be wary of trying it again (as will the other players).

Hot tip

Blind stealing is much more prevalent at the high-limit tables where the monetary value of the blinds bets is much higher. At the micro- and low-limit tables it is much less of an issue and really isn't worth worrying about.

...cont'd

Hot tip

When you're on the small blind, you need only make half a bet as you've already bet the other half in the blind. Don't regard this as a "cheap" bet and make it regardless of your hand. Instead, see it as an opportunity to save half a bet.

The blinds money is irrelevant here; you're making a statement to the other players – namely, that you're not there to be pushed around. However, it must be said that at the low-limit tables where the blinds money is a negligible amount, this is not a major issue. Certainly you don't want to allow yourself to be a pushover, but if you try too hard to defend it, you could end up turning a small loss into a big one. At the high-limit tables, though, it is a completely different matter.

Attacking From the Blinds

By this we mean raising. There are differing opinions as to whether you should raise from the blinds. Ours is that you should do it only with A-A and K-K.

The usual reason to raise pre-flop is when you have a top hand and want to knock out the opposition to increase the chances of it winning. However, by doing this from the blinds (remember, you are last, or next to last, to act), you will be increasing the size of the pot, and thus the pot odds (particularly if you are re-raised by another player).

Far from knocking out the opposition, this will actually give them an incentive to stay in because those with drawing hands may now be getting good odds. In this situation, your top hand is quite likely to lose, and so your pre-flop raise could well turn out to be an expensive one.

With anything other than A-A and K-K, you will usually be better off calling and seeing what develops on the flop.

Stealing the Blinds

Is it worth doing this yourself considering the trifling sums involved? On low-limit tables, the answer is no. Firstly, your bet will probably be called. Remember, low-limit players tend to be much more reckless than high-limit players. Secondly, those trifling sums really aren't worth the bother. On high-limit tables, however, where the blind money is much higher, it can be a good tactic against tight players.

Common Pre-Flop Mistakes

Poor Start Card Selection
This is the most common mistake of all. Quite simply, if you consistently play hands other than the ones in the table on page 52, you are destined to be a big loser.

Calling When You Should be Raising
When you hit the top hands, you have your best opportunity of beating the opposition. By calling and checking, you are letting them see cards cheaply. The more cards you allow them to see, the weaker your top hand becomes.

Slow-Playing
Slow-playing to build the pot has its place but not at the pre-flop stage. You only do this after the flop when you have the nuts, or close to it. Doing it pre-flop just gives the opposition the opportunity to stay in the game and make a better hand than yours when the flop cards are dealt.

Not "Listening" to Your Opponents
Every single action taken by your opponents is telling you something. When they raise, it's usually because they have a big hand. When they check, it's usually because they have a weak or marginal hand. If they check-raise, they're often trying to deceive you. If players who usually act quickly take a long time to throw in a raise, they're trying to make you think they have a weak hand. Listen to what they are telling you and act accordingly.

Playing Hands Out of Position
Playing certain types of hand in the wrong position at the table can get you into serious trouble in the later stages of a game.

Not Taking Advantage of Late Table Position
Being the last, or one of the last, to act puts you in a commanding position. You have an opportunity to play hands that are unplayable in any other position, you can make a move on the blinds money, you can get a free community card, and you are in the best position to increase the size of the pot by raising (see bottom margin note).

Playing the Flop

The flop is the most important stage in the game. It's at this point that you discover just how good, or potentially good, your hand really is. With the three flop cards and your two start cards, you have 71% of your final hand. The significance of this is that, more often than not, seeing the turn and river cards will not improve your hand further. Usually, the hand you have at the flop is the best hand you are going to make. Realizing this fact will save you many lost bets chasing turn and river cards that don't come.

Once you've seen the flop cards, you have many more things to consider than you did pre-flop. These include:

- The strength of your hand, and its potential strength, i.e. the best hand that you are likely to make with it

- The best hand that your opponents are likely to make

- The number of players left in the game

- The players themselves (tight, loose, aggressive, etc.)

- Your opponents' actions before the flop

- The pot odds

The first thing to establish is what sort of hand you have and its potential for improvement. Let's see what you should be looking for with the aid of a sample hand:

Hot tip

A common saying is that if the flop fits (improves your hand), bet, and if it doesn't, fold. Generally, this is good advice. Remember, more often than not, drawing the turn and river cards will not improve your hand further.

Start Cards   Flop Cards

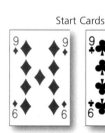    

Your start cards are 9d-9c. The flop is Kc-Qs-As. As things stand, your best hand is 9-9.

With two more cards to come, realistic possibilities are a two-pair or a set (9-9-9). There is also an outside chance of a 9-T-J-Q-K inside straight.

Now let's look at these cards from your opponents' perspective. With A-K-Q on the board, someone almost certainly already has a high pair and, quite possibly, two high pairs. There is a good chance that someone will make a T-J-Q-K-A straight, and if anyone is holding two spades, a spade flush is also a strong possibility.

How does your hand stack up against your opponents'? Forget the 9-9, it's beaten already. If you get another 9 to make a set, this increases the possibility of an opponent making a 9-T-J-Q-K straight. If the 9 is a spade then it's quite likely that one of them will also make a spade flush. So while a 9 will improve your hand, it will very likely make a bigger hand for an opponent. Another ace, king or queen would give you two pairs. However, any of these could well give an opponent a set. So whichever way you look at it, this hand is a non-starter.

An important factor when evaluating the flop is the number of opponents still in. The fewer you are facing, the more chance you have of winning with a hand that's not so good. An example would be a middle pair, e.g. 8-8. Against three or more opponents, it stands little chance; against one, or even two, it could hold up.

How your opponents play also needs to be considered. With cautious players who rarely raise, it can be worth trying one more bet to see the next card. If there's an aggressive player behind you though, who's likely to raise, folding will probably save you a bet.

You should also be aware of what your opponents were doing pre-flop. Someone who was raising probably had a high pair or an A-K. If the flop turns up high cards, they will probably now be on a set, or a two-pair. More raises should have you folding.

Hot tip

If your best hand at the flop is a low to middle pair and there are overcards (particularly high ones) on the board, fold the hand. The only exception is if the pot is large enough to warrant trying to hit a set.

Don't forget

One of the most important factors in deciding whether to play after the flop is the number of opponents. The more there are, the better your hand has to be.

Playing Pairs on the Flop

The main considerations when playing pairs are overcards and kickers. If the overcards are on the board (against you), then you are at an immediate disadvantage. If you have a low kicker to go with the pair, you are at even more of a disadvantage. For example:

Start Cards

Flop Cards

Your start cards are Q-Q and the hand was looking good until the flop brought the king overcard. Your best move here is to raise and see how the opposition respond. If you are re-raised, you can assume someone has a K in their hand or has hit something even better, and thus fold. If your raise is called, see the hand out as cheaply as possible but fold to any subsequent raises assuming your hand doesn't improve. Don't forget: Q-Q looks nice but it is just a pair and is easily beaten. Another example:

When playing pairs after the flop, you must bear in mind that they are not strong hands even if the flop looks safe. Bets from tight players should have you dropping them like hot bricks. Against loose players, they are worth playing. As ever, knowing your opponents is a major factor when deciding what hands to play.

Start Cards

Flop Cards

You hold Jd-2d and were hoping to see more diamonds on the flop to give you a flush draw. Instead, you've picked up another jack with no overcards. Still pretty good, you may say. Well, that depends on whether you're a gambler or a poker player. If it's the former, this is a good hand to gamble on. With a safe-looking flop, you do have a fair chance of winning.

If you're playing poker, though, it's not so good as there's an equally fair chance that you won't win. You may have two jacks, but you also have a very low kicker. If four or five players are still in, the chances are good that one of them will also have a jack, but with a higher kicker, or a better hand.

This is a classic example of a hand that is shaping up to be the second-best one, and you should fold if there is any serious betting action. Against one or two opponents, you could call and see what develops. A final example:

Here, you have 7-7 with an eight kicker. You have an overcard against you and no chance of a flush or a straight, plus there are two diamonds on the board giving an opponent a possible flush. Your only prospect is hitting another 7 for a set. This hand is junk – dump it.

A slightly different flop, though, makes the hand playable. With two clubs on the board, you need just one more for a flush.

With two ways of making a good hand (a flush and a set), you now have a reasonable drawing hand.

Beware

Playing pairs with a low kicker will get you into trouble time and time again.

Hot tip

Not knowing when to let go of pairs is a mistake made by far too many players. If the flop doesn't hit them, these are "play and pray" hands.

Two Pairs on the Flop

These can fall in one of two ways: boarded, where one of the pairs is on the board and the other is in the player's hand, or split, where one card of each pair is in the player's hand.

The Boarded Two-Pair

Start Cards | Flop Cards

Your start cards are J-J and the flop turns up K-K-5 to give you two pairs. This is a boarded two-pair. There are three likely scenarios here:

1) Everybody has the pair on the board. So any other players who are holding a pocket pair also have a two-pair. If one of them has a pocket pair higher than yours, he or she is in the driving seat

2) None of your opponents has a pocket pair. Assuming none of them is holding a king either, you are top-dog at the moment

3) Another player is holding a king and thus has a set (and possibly a five as well for a full house)

So how do you play this hand? Well, the first thing to note is that with two kings already out, there is less chance of an opponent holding another one. Nevertheless, it is still a good possibility and you need to find out now before the bets double.

Therefore, you raise. If you get re-raised, you can assume the re-raiser has a third king and thus fold. If your opponents don't have a king, they are going to think that you have it because you've raised, and will fold themselves. If you get called, the caller could be slow-playing. Be wary.

The Split Two-Pair

In this scenario, the pairs are split between your start cards and the board, as shown below:

Start Cards   Flop Cards

A split two-pair is a much stronger hand than a boarded two-pair as there is no pair on the board. This hand can be a killer as there's no way an opponent can put you on it.

That said, don't lose sight of the fact that a split pair is still only the second-worst hand. It is beaten by sets, straights, flushes, full houses and quads. The advice, therefore, is to play it aggressively by raising to make the opposition fold – slow-playing it could cause you a lot of grief at the end.

However, if there are still players in at the turn, and the turn card indicates a possible set, flush, or straight for someone, you need to back off.

For example:

Start Cards   Flop Cards

If the turn card is a heart, a flush for an opponent is now a definite possibility. If someone now raises, throw in the towel. Otherwise, just call; you've still got a good chance to win this hand, so if you can see the final card for one more bet, it's worth doing.

Playing Sets on the Flop

As with the two-pair, these hands fall in one of two ways – two cards in the pocket and one on the board (concealed), or two cards on the board and one in the pocket (open).

While sets are an excellent hand (particularly concealed sets), they are far from being unbeatable. Many players slow-play this hand hoping to get as much money in the pot as possible. In some situations this can be the correct play, however, usually it is incorrect as they are leaving themselves open to the risk of someone completing a drawing hand. The general rule, therefore, is that sets are played in the same way as pairs and two-pairs – aggressively.

Concealed Set

Of the two, concealed sets are by far the more powerful. If two of the cards are in the pocket, and only one is on the board, the opposition will have no idea that you have one. Let's look at a couple of examples of how to play them.

Start Cards   Flop Cards

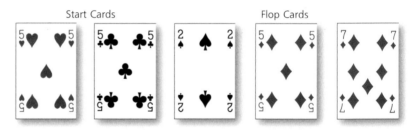

You've got 5-5 and another 5 on the board for your set. Otherwise, the flop is far from ideal. A bad card on the turn or river could bring a straight or a flush for an opponent. In either case, your set loses.

Therefore, you've got to force these players out of the hand by raising, thus making it too expensive for them to continue. If your raise is called, re-raise to keep the pressure on. Don't call – that will get you nowhere.

However, if the turn brings another low/middle card or diamond, or even worse, a low diamond, you will have to play the hand out by checking and calling. If you are raised, you should fold.

Hot tip

Tempting though it may be, it is very rarely correct to slow-play a set. Yet, this is just what many players do. You will hear them bewailing their bad luck – "Two sets in a row and beaten on the river each time". This isn't bad luck; it's bad play. They should have raised the opposition out of the game before the river.

...cont'd

Here's an example of when it can be correct to slow-play a set.

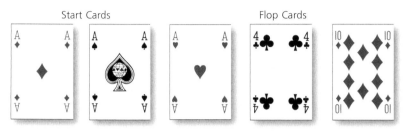

Start Cards   Flop Cards

You've hit the highest set. Furthermore, there is little likelihood of being beaten by a straight or a flush. That said, two more high cards, or two more low cards, on the turn and the river could give an opponent a straight. Similarly, another two diamonds could see someone hitting a flush.

These are both long shots though, and you will be very unlucky to lose this hand. Assuming you have only one or two opponents, you can slow-play and trust that nothing dangerous falls on the turn and river. With three or more opponents, you would *not* slow-play; it would be too risky.

Open Set
This hand is good, but not nearly as good as a concealed set.

Start Cards   Flop Cards

You have three kings for your set but a low kicker. An opponent holding the fourth king and another card, four or above, also has the same set but with a higher kicker. You could be beaten here already. Nevertheless, with a hand this good, you need to see some evidence. Raise. An opponent who does have a king is going to come straight back with a re-raise. In this case, you should probably fold.

67

Hot tip

The only time you would slow-play a set on the flop is when the set is a high one, the board cards offer little chance of a straight or a flush, and you have no more than two opponents.

Hot tip

This example is a good illustration of how the raise is used to gain information about an opponent's hand.

Flush Draws on the Flop

When a player's pocket cards are suited the chance of hitting a flush is suddenly on. Knowing how powerful this hand is, many players will draw to the river in the hope of getting it. In most cases, though, they are making a mistake. It is a fact that consistently making this play represents a major leak in most players' games.

The first thing to be aware of is that you simply cannot play *any* suited cards. This is because the odds against making the flush are 16 to 1. The following is a typical example of a hand that should not be played.

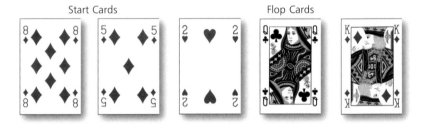

You've been dealt 8d-5d giving you a chance of a diamond flush. The flop cards are 2h-Qc-Kd, which gives you three diamonds. You need both the turn and river cards to be diamonds as well, and the chances of this happening are 1 in 23. So, effectively, you can discount the flush.

What else do you have? If you get an 8 or a 5, you've only got a low pair. Also, there's no prospect of a straight. This hand was a loser right from the beginning. Let's see another example:

Here you kicked off with a top hand: Ac-Kc.

As regards the flush, the flop has not been helpful; you still need two more clubs – the same 1 in 23 long-shot as in our first example. However, you've flopped the top pair with a king kicker, and also a nut four-to-a-straight draw.

Although you've missed the flush draw, you still have two more good options. The lesson, then, is that you only play suited pocket cards if they are either connected, or high cards (both, ideally). This gives you other options should you miss the flush, which you usually will.

Another example:

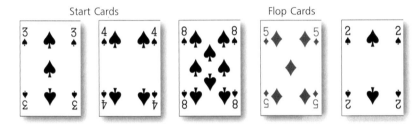

Start Cards   Flop Cards

Your start cards are 3s-4s. The flop brings two more spades to give you a good chance of hitting the flush.

The problem is that even if you make it, it is only going to be a 4 high flush. If another player also makes the flush, his or hers will almost certainly be better than yours. Therefore, you will have to play this one aggressively to force out any players who have spades in their hands. While it probably won't work, as most players will always try to hit a flush, it's the only thing you can do.

If the turn or river does bring another spade to complete your flush and an opponent starts raising, then you can be fairly sure that this player has a higher flush than yours. In this case, you will have to consider folding. If you do play, just call the raise, don't re-raise.

Don't forget

Never play suited cards unless they are either high cards, or are connected. By doing this, if you miss the flush, you will still have other ways to hit a good hand.

Straight Draws on the Flop

A straight is a powerful hand, and as with flush draws, it is common to see people playing them to the river in the hope of hitting one. However, straights are not as good as flushes, so even if you hit one, it may well not be the winning hand. One big danger with straights is hitting one on the low end and not being aware of (or forgetting) the possibility of someone hitting the high end. For example:

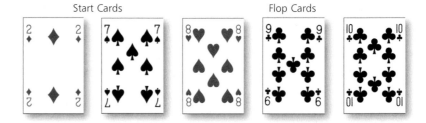

Start Cards · Flop Cards

You have 7-8-9-T, and need a 6 or a J to complete the straight. However, if you do get it, it will be the low end of the straight. An opponent with J-Q (which is quite likely as they are high cards) will have a higher straight. In a situation like this you have to be careful – just call or check. If someone raises, fold. If you do get the straight on the turn or river, raise to see where you are. If you are re-raised, you can be fairly sure someone has hit the high end. Fold.

Start Cards · Flop Cards

Here, you've flopped a nut straight. With a king and a queen on the board, there is a good chance that someone will hit a high pair, or better still, a high two-pair. If they do, you are likely to get some serious action. With nothing likely to beat your straight, you can slow-play; just check and call. You want someone to hit a hand here.

Backdoor straight draws are hands that require both the turn and the river card to fall favourably. Below we see an outside backdoor straight draw. It requires A-5 to complete:

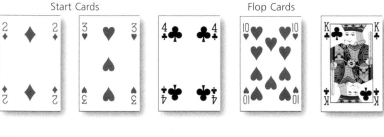

Here we see an inside backdoor straight draw. It requires J-K to complete it:

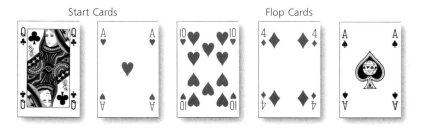

The odds of hitting an outside backdoor straight are 1 in 38, and they are 1 in 71 for the inside backdoor straight. Not good. Therefore, in most cases you should dump these hands unceremoniously. The only time you might play them is when they also have other possibilities. For example, the inside straight draw above where the hand also has A-A with a queen kicker.

At the risk of repeating ourselves, the most important thing to remember with drawing hands, be they straights, flushes, or sets, is that the pot odds must be high enough to make the play profitable over the long term. In most cases, this requires a good number of players to be in the hand; if you get to the flop and have only one or two opponents, the odds just won't be there.

Don't forget

Drawing hands are best played from a late position. This allows you to fold pre-flop if most of the opposition has already done so. Remember, you need plenty of opponents for these hands to be profitable.

Drawing Hands/Pot Odds

Here, we'll show two examples to demonstrate the importance of pot odds when playing drawing hands. You are playing at a ten-seat $1.00/2.00 fixed-limit table, and holding Jd-8d. Five players fold and the other four bet. You call. This puts five bets into the pot – $5.

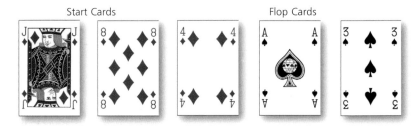

Start Cards   Flop Cards

Don't forget

If you are in a marginal situation with regard to the pot odds, don't forget to factor in the implied odds (see page 42).

72

The flop cards are dealt. Two players bet and the other two fold. This puts two more dollars in the pot – it now stands at $7. It's your turn to bet; what do you do? The only good hand you're likely to make with these cards is a diamond flush. The chance of hitting it, though, is 1 in 23. The pot odds are 7:1 ($7 in the pot divided by the $1 you need to call). The odds against hitting the flush are much higher than the pot odds, so you fold.

You are sitting at the same $1.00/2.00 table, and this time holding 8h-9c. Two players fold; the others, including you, all bet. This puts $8 in the pot. Then the flop is dealt.

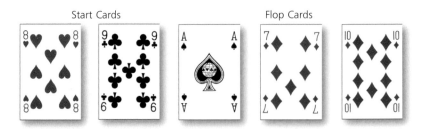

Start Cards   Flop Cards

Four players fold, one raises, and two call the raise. The pot now stands at $14. You have an outside straight draw, a 5-1 shot. The pot odds are 7:1 ($14 pot divided by the $2 you need to call the raise). The odds against making your hand are lower than the pot odds so it's correct to bet.

Playing a Flush or Straight on the Flop

Once in a blue moon, you will have the good fortune to flop a flush or a straight. The first thing to be aware of is that you haven't cracked it yet. While these two hands win most of the time, they don't always. How you play them depends on the strength of the hand and the flop cards.
For example:

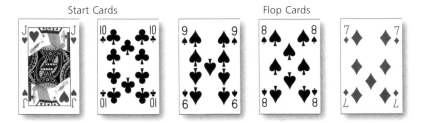

Start Cards · Flop Cards

You've caught the high end of a straight. However, the two spades could be giving someone a flush draw. Therefore, you have to play this aggressively in order to force out anyone holding spades by raising. If you are re-raised, re-raise the raiser. If another spade does come though, then see the hand out as cheaply as possible.

In the example below, you have a queen high flush. However, an opponent with the ace or king of diamonds needs just one more diamond to make a higher flush.

Start Cards · Flop Cards

It would be pointless raising in this situation, as with two cards still to come and a chance of hitting a high flush, one extra bet is unlikely to make anyone fold. Therefore, you may as well slow-play it and hope for the best.

Hot tip

In the example opposite, the situation would be completely different if you were playing at a no-limit table. Then you could put in a really big bet so that the opposition would have to pay dearly to see the next card.

Overcards on the Flop

This is a situation where one, or both, of your pocket cards are higher than any card on the board. For example:

Start Cards   Flop Cards

You have Ad-9d, and were hoping for a high pair or a flush draw on the flop. Instead, all you've got is one overcard. What do you do now?

First, if you do play the hand and hit a pair, that's all you'll have – just a pair. If it's a nine, you will be beaten by an opponent holding a queen. Second, the board is showing a possible flush draw. So with two ways of being beaten even if you make a pair, you would have to fold. Note that this is usually the safest option with overcards.

However, if certain conditions are met, it can be correct to play overcards. For example:

Start Cards   Flop Cards

Here you have two overcards, either of which can make a top pair. The jack on the board also gives you an outside chance of a straight. Furthermore, the flop is safe in that it offers no straight or flush possibilities to the opposition.

In these conditions, and against one or two opponents, it would be worth playing.

Full House on the Flop

A full house is a wonderful hand – usually. Sometimes, though, they are not so good. Consider the following:

Start Cards   Flop Cards

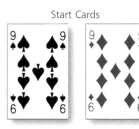   

Beware

Be very wary of a full house when the set part of it is on the board, and is higher than the pair in your hand. A player with a higher pair will have a higher full house.

You have three jacks and two nines. However, this is not as good a hand as it seems, and the reason is that the three jacks are all on the board. Thus every player still in the game has them as well. Effectively, all you actually have is the pair of nines, and you would have to play the hand on this basis, as any player with a higher pair will beat you.

All you can do here is to raise in an attempt to knock out opponents with high cards that can make a higher pair than your 9-9. If you are re-raised, you are almost certainly up against another pair. It might be higher than yours or it might be lower, so you will have to play the hand out by checking and calling. You can't fold as you may well have the winning hand, but nor do you want to put any more in the pot than you have to, as you also have a fair chance of losing.

Another example:

Start Cards   Flop Cards

This full house is much better. With a jack in your start cards, quads are impossible. The hand is not unbeatable – an opponent with the last jack could still make a higher pair than 9-9, but in reality, it's very unlikely.

Hot tip

Say your start cards were 9-J and the board was 9-9-J. This full house would be much weaker than the one opposite as an opponent with two jacks and any other pair would beat you. In this situation, you would have to play aggressively to deny opponents the chance of doing it.

Playing the Turn

As a general rule, if you haven't completed your hand by this stage, you should fold. By continuing, you are usually throwing good money after bad. However, if you have, and have been playing the correct start cards, it should be the best hand, or close to it. If you are confident that it is, you should now be raising to get money in the pot. If you are re-raised, though, take a time-out to re-evaluate your hand and the board, checking that you haven't missed something. If you still can't see any obvious danger, re-raise the raiser. This is also likely to force out players who are hoping to complete a drawing hand on the river. Remember, this is your last chance to do this.

Aggressiveness at this stage is the best policy. Many players will fold good hands when faced with a bombardment of raises and re-raises. Think of it in this way: if you've been playing correctly by playing only good start cards, and from the correct positions, you will have saved yourself a large number of single bets. What you are doing now is investing some of those bets on a good hand when it really counts.

The only times you should check or call are:

- When you are drawing to a flush, straight or set

- When you've missed the hand you wanted and ended up with something not quite so good. For example, you may have been aiming at the high end of a straight and, instead, hit the low end. Whatever, if you aren't confident the hand is going to win but think it has a chance, play it out by calling and checking. Don't pay any more than you have to, though

- When you have a nut hand. In this case, slow-play the hand to ensure as many of your opponents as possible stay in to the end. You want to give them every opportunity to hit their hands

Playing the River

When the river card flips over, you know for sure what your best hand is. In most cases, though, it will be no better than it was on the turn, or even the flop. If you've been drawing to a flush or straight because the pot odds warranted it, you now either have it or you don't. Your decision is clear-cut: bet or fold (against one opponent, it may be worth trying to bluff the other player out of it by raising).

If you already had your best hand on the turn and were betting aggressively, re-evaluate the board with regard to how the river card may have improved your opponents' hands. Things to take note of are:

- A third suit, indicating that a flush is possible. If a player who was previously calling and checking now puts in a raise, this is the time to either fold a straight or lower, or just call

- A pair on the board. In this situation, you may now be up against a set, a full house, or quads. If an opponent raises and you hold nothing better than a pair, fold. Otherwise, call

- A card that connects other board cards. This increases the possibility of a straight. Of course, if you already have a straight beaten, you're going to love this

A good rule for river play is that you should rarely fold a hand that has a reasonable chance of winning. If in doubt, just call and check to see the hand out cheaply, but don't fold it unless someone is raising aggressively. Surrendering a winning hand is not a smart move.

Be wary of getting involved in a raising war with two or more opponents when you are holding nothing higher than a pair. It's very tempting to play a pair of aces to the end, but against two opponents who are betting aggressively, it's usually a costly mistake. In this situation, you will almost always be beaten by a two-pair or a set.

Hot tip

A raise on the river indicates that the player has either hit a good hand and is confident of winning, or has a weak one and is trying to bluff his/her way out of trouble.

This is where player observation pays off. Unless you are holding a strong hand yourself, against a tight-passive player who rarely raises, you should probably fold. Against an aggressive or loose player, re-raise with a strong hand. Otherwise, just call.

Beware

Never get involved in a heavily contested multi-way pot if you are holding only a pair. Don't forget, even if it's a high pair, it's still the weakest of all the poker hands.

Short-Hand Play

Playing short-hand is when you face six opponents or fewer. This can be at a ten-seat table where several seats are unoccupied, a six-seat, or a two-seat table. Whichever, the fact that you are facing fewer opponents means that you must adjust your strategy accordingly.

With less opposition, hands take on a higher value. Many games are won with a pair, or a two-pair. Many start cards that you would fold in a ten-player game are worth playing short-hand. Middle pairs (7-7 to T-T) should be played in the same way as you would play high pairs at a ten-seat table. Also, kickers are less of an issue as the chances of an opponent having a higher card are lower.

Drawing hands, however, are much less valuable. The reason is that with fewer opponents, the pot odds are often not high enough to warrant playing these hands. Thus, you should only play connectors and suited cards that have a high face value, giving you the chance of a high pair as well; middle and low cards should be folded. Because of this, don't let a straight or flush draw on the board put you off playing a good pair or two-pair. The chances of being beaten by a drawing hand are much less than in a ten-player game.

A very important factor in short-handed poker is your style of play. Aggression is the keyword. Players who call frequently will find it tough going as they are going to find themselves being raised constantly.

Bluffing is a much used tactic in short-hand poker and you need to be able to deal with this – if you allow yourself to be intimidated, you will lose many pots to players with lesser hands.

You also need to be aware of the danger of being beaten by the blinds. These come round much more quickly than in a ten-player game, and players who sit and wait for the best hands are going to lose a lot of their money in the blinds. Thus, you will need to win pots more frequently, which in turn means playing more hands.

Texas Hold'em Odds

Start Card Probabilities

The table below shows the statistical probability of being dealt the types of hand you need to win at Texas Hold'em:

Hand	Odds
A-A or K-K	110 : 1
A-A, K-K or Q-Q	73 : 1
A-A, K-K, Q-Q or J-J	54 : 1
A-A, K-K, Q-Q, J-J or T-T	43 : 1
A-K suited	331 : 1
A-K unsuited	110 : 1
K-Q suited	331 : 1
K-Q unsuited	110 : 1
A single ace	5.25 : 1
Suited cards	3.2 : 1
Connected cards, suited	24 : 1
Connected cards, unsuited	5 : 1
Pair	16 : 1

Hot tip

How does this table help you in the course of a hand? The answer is it doesn't. What it does do is make it very plain what loose players must be playing with.

So the next time you have a medium pair and a maniac raises you, raise him right back instead of folding.

This shows very clearly that the really good hands – high pairs and two high cards, do not come around too often, and demonstrates why the majority of the hands you are dealt should be folded – at least 80% of them at a ten-seat table. It is also an eye-opener regarding the types of hand that really loose players get involved with. These players will play most hands and the table tells you that they must be betting on rubbish the majority of the time.

By having the discipline to wait for a good hand, nine times out of ten, you will have a big advantage over them.

...cont'd

Probability Of Making Specific Hands

This table shows how likely you are to complete the most common hands in Texas Hold'em:

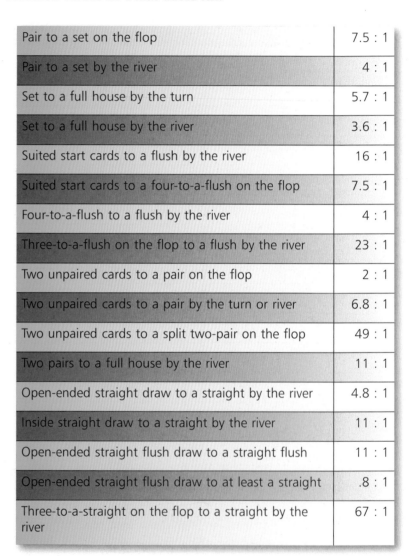

Pair to a set on the flop	7.5 : 1
Pair to a set by the river	4 : 1
Set to a full house by the turn	5.7 : 1
Set to a full house by the river	3.6 : 1
Suited start cards to a flush by the river	16 : 1
Suited start cards to a four-to-a-flush on the flop	7.5 : 1
Four-to-a-flush to a flush by the river	4 : 1
Three-to-a-flush on the flop to a flush by the river	23 : 1
Two unpaired cards to a pair on the flop	2 : 1
Two unpaired cards to a pair by the turn or river	6.8 : 1
Two unpaired cards to a split two-pair on the flop	49 : 1
Two pairs to a full house by the river	11 : 1
Open-ended straight draw to a straight by the river	4.8 : 1
Inside straight draw to a straight by the river	11 : 1
Open-ended straight flush draw to a straight flush	11 : 1
Open-ended straight flush draw to at least a straight	.8 : 1
Three-to-a-straight on the flop to a straight by the river	67 : 1

Knowing how likely you are to make a specific hand is extremely useful when faced with a judgement call. If you can get to grips with pot odds as well, you will be well on the way to being a successful poker player.

Hot tip

If you can commit this table to memory and use it in conjunction with pot odds, you will nearly always know when to play and when to fold.

6 No-Limit Texas Hold'em Strategy

While the basic concepts of good strategy such as correct start card selection, apply to both fixed-limit and no-limit poker, there are a range of other factors you need to know about with regard to no-limit.

82 Introduction

83 Start Cards

84 Pre-Flop Strategy

87 Post-Flop Strategy

88 The All-In Bet

89 Bluffing

90 Trapping

91 Stack Size

92 Common No-Limit Mistakes

Introduction

No-limit poker gives players complete freedom of choice regarding the size of the bets they make. If they want to risk their entire stack on one bet, they can. This single factor introduces a number of elements that makes no-limit a much more difficult game to master. These include:

Skill
Because bets can be huge, no-limit provides little room for error. Consistently bad play (or bad luck) can bankrupt you in a very short space of time. Consequently, you need to be a far more proficient player to survive in this game.

Psychology
The ever-present threat of being suddenly faced with a huge bet to stay in the game can have a dramatic influence on some players' behavior. Some will fold winning hands rather than get into a confrontation with an aggressive opponent.

Stack Size
A player with a stack twenty times the size of yours can keep going all-in against you with trash hands. Even if the first few miss, eventually your opponent is going to pull a lucky card and bust you. There is simply no defence against this. If you keep folding, in many cases you will be folding the winning hand, and if you bet, the player will get you in the end. This is a bit of a simplification but it serves to illustrate the point – players with a small stack are at a big disadvantage.

Bluffing
In fixed-limit, the bluff is a weak play as it costs only a small bet to call it. In no-limit, it is a powerful weapon that wins many pots with inferior hands. Knowing how, and when, to use the bluff is a distinguishing feature of the good no-limit player.

Aggression/Initiative
The player in control of the betting, i.e. making the big bets, has the initiative; opponents are responding to his or her actions and are usually on the back foot.

Hot tip

If you like excitement, no-limit is the game for you. There's no denying that fixed-limit can be a drudge. In no-limit, you can double (or lose) your stack in a single hand.

Start Cards

Start card requirements for no-limit are slightly different from those in fixed-limit, and one reason for this is the fact that drawing hands have less value. Playing these hands will have you folding to a large bet far more than in low-limit because it will be too expensive to continue with the hand.

Also, very often no-limit games don't get as far as the river (or even the turn) due to the volatility of the betting. Very often, anyone playing suited or connected start cards in the hope of making a straight or a flush won't get a chance to complete it, and thus will have wasted their bets. Consequently, playing this type of hand can be expensive in no-limit. A lot depends on the opposition; if they are mainly the passive type, drawing hands can be worth playing. It only takes one or two aggressive players, though, to make playing drawing hands a very risky exercise.

There is also the risk of being tempted to call a large bet due to inexperience, or simply making a mistake. In fixed-limit it won't be too costly; in no-limit it may be very expensive, particularly if you then make the second-best hand and decide to play on with it. This is what's known as being "trapped" and it usually stems from poor start card selection.

The following table lists the recommended start cards for no-limit Hold'em:

Don't forget

Flush and straight draws are not as good in no-limit as they are in fixed-limit. You will have less chance to complete them, and even if you do, the pot odds will often not be high enough to make them pay over the long term.

Hot tip

Sticking to the start cards in the table opposite will keep you out of many awkward and, potentially, dangerous situations.

Playable Start Cards
Early Position
A-A, K-K, Q-Q, A-Ks, A-Qs, A-Ko, A-Qo
Middle Position
J-J, T-T, 9-9, A-Js, A-Ts, K-Qs, K-Js, Q-Js, A-Jo, A-To, K-Qo, K-Jo, plus all the early position hands
Late Position
8-8, 7-7, 6-6, 5-5, 4-4, 3-3, 2-2, A-5s, A-4s, A-3s, A-2s, K-Ts, K-9s, Q-Ts, J-Ts, K-To, Q-Jo, Q-To, plus early and middle position hands
A – Ace, K – King, Q – Queen, J – Jack, T – Ten, 2-9 – card value, x – unknown card, s – same suit, o – different suits

Pre-Flop Strategy

The big danger in no-limit is getting yourself trapped with the second-best hand. Remember, the more money you commit to a pot, the harder it becomes to write it off; you will always be tempted to see just one more card in the hope of improving your hand. This is fatal in no-limit. It's going to happen of course, but by playing only the right start cards, you will be limiting the times it does.

Early Position

Playable hands are: A-A, K-K, Q-Q, A-Ks, A-Ko, A-Qs, A-Qo.

With A-A to Q-Q, you bet hard. These are top hands pre-flop but are more likely to be beaten the longer the game goes on. As in fixed-limit, the goal is to knock out as much of the competition pre-flop as possible.

How much do you raise by, though? Some players would go all in with A-A hoping one opponent will accept the challenge. In this situation, they would be a hot favorite to win the pot. You can do this yourself – it's not a bad play; only do it with A-A, though. What's more likely to happen, however, is that everyone will simply fold; all you'll have won is the blinds money, which is not much reward for the best hand. What you want to do then is bet an amount that will get all but one or two of your opponents out of the game. Typically, this will be four or five times the size of the higher betting limit ($80-100 in a $10.00/20.00 game). This will make most players fold.

If you are re-raised by a large amount, fold anything lower than K-K. With A-A or K-K, re-raise the raiser. If the re-raise is low, call with Q-Q. If someone goes all-in, or a second player re-raises, fold everything bar A-A.

With A-Ks, A-Ko, A-Qs and A-Qo, just bet and see what develops. A small raise you can call with A-Ks and A-Ko. Fold the A-Qs and A-Qo. Fold all these hands to a large raise.

Middle Position

Playable hands are: J-J, T-T, 9-9, A-Js, A-Ts, K-Qs, K-Js, Q-Js, A-Jo, A-To, K-Qo, K-Jo, plus all the early position hands.

In middle position, you should play A-A, K-K, Q-Q in exactly the same way you would in early position. You can also raise with J-J, T-T, 9-9, A-Ks, A-Ko, A-Qs and A-Qo. Quite apart from limiting the competition, you will also be buying yourself a better table position.

If your J-J to 9-9 is re-raised, re-raise the raiser. You really need to win with these hands before the flop, as afterwards they will be vulnerable to overcards. If your opponent(s) persist and re-raise yet again, you are probably beaten and should fold. While these are good cards and you should make a decent attempt to win the pot with them, you should back down in the face of determined opposition.

With A-Ks, A-Ko, A-Qs and A-Qo, you should fold to any re-raise. The lesser hands, from A-Js downwards, are worth seeing the flop with if you can do so cheaply by calling and checking. These often turn into high pairs and high two-pairs. In the face of any raises, you should fold them, though.

Late Position

Playable hands are: 8-8, 7-7, 6-6, 5-5, 4-4, 3-3, 2-2, A-5s, A-4s, A-3s, A-2s, K-Ts, K-9s, Q-Ts, J-Ts, K-To, Q-Jo, Q-To, plus all the early and middle position hands.

In late position, you have the big advantage of having seen all your opponents' moves. This allows you to play many more hands than you would in the earlier positions.

Play A-A to 9-9 as already described. With these hands, you are looking to tempt one opponent into calling your bet and then re-raise that player out of the game. The goal is to win the pot then and there.

In no-limit, low and middle pairs are more valuable than they are in fixed-limit (see bottom margin note).

Hot tip

Making a large bet from a middle position will often buy you a better table position for the later betting rounds. In no-limit this is a much more effective strategy than it is in fixed-limit.

Hot tip

Because it is less common to see straights and flushes in no-limit, low and middle pairs that can turn into a set are worth more than they are in fixed-limit.

...cont'd

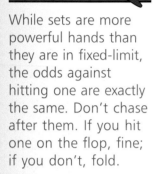

The reason for this is that straights and flushes are less common in no-limit as the pot odds are often not good enough to make them worth playing. With low and middle pairs, you are looking to hit a set. These hands (particularly concealed sets) are the ideal hands in no-limit and win huge pots.

Some people advocate raising pre-flop with any pair to build up the pot in case the set hits. However, you must remember that the chance of making this hand on the flop from a pair is 1 in 7.5. Bearing this in mind, you're probably better off seeing the flop as cheaply as possible with middle and low pairs. If there's a small raise in front of you, call, but fold to a large raise, or a re-raise.

Notice that we do not advise playing low or middle connectors, suited or otherwise. These are drawing hands, and as previously stated, the pot odds, generally, do not allow you to make a profit with them.

A-2s to A-5s are worth playing, as not only do they give you a chance of a straight or a flush, you can also hit a top pair. Plus, if you hit a low pair or set, you'll have the highest kicker.

Pre-Flop Tips

Bets need to be substantial. If you're attempting to knock out the opposition, either to win the pot outright or to limit the competition, pre-flop bets need to be significant in comparison to the pot. You must present your opponents with a powerful incentive to fold. Half-hearted attempts that fail often have repercussions in the later stages of the game.

Try trapping an opponent. The usual procedure with A-A or K-K is to raise immediately. Do the opposite once in a while by just calling. Then, assuming you get a safe flop, throw in a large bet. Hopefully, one opponent will have hit a high pair and will call or even re-raise. Your initial small bet will probably have him thinking that you have a lower pair or are trying to steal.

Post-Flop Strategy

The mechanics of post-flop play, e.g. reading the board, are no different from those in fixed-limit, so we're not going to repeat ourselves by explaining how to play each type of hand as we did in Chapter 5. Rather, we'll just highlight some pertinent points.

In no-limit, the decisions you make here are far more critical than in fixed-limit as, potentially, there is a lot more at stake.

If you don't think your hand measures up, you've got two choices: either drop it or bet hard (bluff). Calling is not usually a good move in no-limit for the simple reason that it puts no pressure on the opposition – something you should be looking to do as often as possible. The only time you should be calling is when you've flopped a monster hand or are on a draw. If it's the former, you will be slow-playing to let as many players as possible see the turn and river cards and, hopefully, hit a lesser hand.

If you do decide to bluff it out, your decision must be based on the number of your opponents and how they are likely to respond. The more opposition you have, the riskier this move is, so only do it against one or two opponents. They must also be the type who are likely to fold under pressure. If you get it wrong and are called or raised, you have to let the hand go, regardless of how much you have invested in the pot. While this type of play is not going to win every time, what it will do is get you a lot more action when you do have the best hand. If your opponents see that you take risks occasionally, they will be more inclined to call your bets.

Straight and flush draws you should drop if the flop doesn't give you two of the cards you need. Even if it does, you will need to consider the pot odds to determine if it's worthwhile paying to see the turn card.

We mentioned earlier that sets can be a killer hand in no-limit and this is true. However, it is a big mistake to chase them consistently to the turn and river. Generally, if the third card doesn't fall on the flop, fold the hand.

Hot tip

Aggressive bluffing post-flop will steal many pots. However, you must pick players who allow themselves to be bullied. Also, you must be able to let the hand go if the bluff is called.

The All-In Bet

Players go all-in when they put all their money in the pot. This is the most powerful move that can be made in poker.

The tactic is most commonly used in tournaments, often in the latter stages to rebuild a dangerously low stack. Players in this situation are in imminent danger of being swallowed up by the blinds and so need to do something drastic to get back in the game. As soon as they get a half-decent hand, they'll go all-in. They've got little to lose by doing this – if they win they double their stack and are back in the game; if they lose, they're out, which they soon would have been anyway because of the blinds.

Should you call an all-in bet or make one yourself in a cash game, though? In the right circumstances, most definitely. "Right circumstances" would be defined as:

Pre-Flop

With A-A, against any opponent regardless of table position. With K-K, in late position only, assuming: a) no more than one player is all-in (if two players are all-in, you have to assume one of them has A-A), and b) the opponent isn't a tight player (tight players rarely go all-in pre-flop with less than A-A).

Post-Flop

Against any opponent when you are holding a set, assuming: a) it is a concealed set (no pair on the board to give possible quads or a full house to opponents), and b) there is no flush or straight draw on the board.

When you are holding a nut straight, assuming: a) there is no flush draw, and b) the board isn't paired.

When you are holding a nut flush and the board isn't paired. The exception to the above is when a short-stacked player goes all in (see bottom margin note).

Bluffing

In no-limit, the power of the unlimited bet makes bluffing a much more potent weapon. It can also make it a double-edged sword, though; if the bluff is called, you may lose more. Because of this danger, you need to pick the right time and the right opponent – indiscriminate bluffing will get you nowhere. The opponent is probably the most important factor. Aggressive players who don't like backing down, and maniacs who can't resist betting, should not be bluffed. Unless you are prepared to go the whole hog with an all-in bet, they will often call you.

Against tight players, you should only try a bluff if you act after them; you need to see them play first – if they make a good-sized bet then they've hit a good hand and you can forget the idea. If they call or check then go ahead.

The ideal opponent to bluff is the tight-passive player. These people really shouldn't be playing no-limit; they are simply too timid for their own good. Usually, they are more concerned with protecting their stack than they are in building it up.

In no-limit, bluffing can win money in a more roundabout way. Obviously, you can't expect to win every bluff; you are going to get caught out now and again. However, when you do, even though you've lost some money, there is a positive side effect. By showing the opposition that you are prepared to take risks, you are creating a loose (or less tight, at any rate) table image. When you do get the monster hand, the opposition are more likely to call your bets and your big hand will win a lot more money.

The trick is not to lose money overall on the bluffs. Even if you just break even on them (and by carefully selecting the opponents to bluff, you should achieve at least that), your winnings on the big hands will be increased considerably.

Being seen as a timid player is the worst table image you can have in no-limit. The occasional bluff will prevent this and make the opposition treat you with much more respect.

Hot tip

Essentially, a bluff is playing the opponent rather than the cards. You are gambling that your perception of other players is accurate. If it is, and they fold, the cards are irrelevant.

Hot tip

Being caught out with a bluff occasionally is not a bad thing as it will induce opponents to take more chances against you.

Beware

Certain hands have a much greater potential than others for trapping players. Any high card with a low card (A-4, K-3, for example), particularly if unsuited, is liable to make only a second- or third-best hand.

Hot tip

Trap hands are known as "dominated hands" because of the likelihood of an opponent having a similar but better one. For example, you have A-5 and an opponent has A-Q. Your A-5 is dominated because you need to hit at least a pair to win. The A-Q, however, will win without any improvement.

Trapping

This is when you think you have the winning hand but an opponent has an even better hand. Because you expect to win, you keep betting; by the time the truth begins to dawn, it's too late. If you fold, you have to surrender all the money you've put in the pot; if you continue you're going to lose even more – you've trapped yourself in a no-win situation.

In most cases, players trap themselves rather than being trapped deliberately by an opponent. This is usually the result of playing bad start cards. For example, you play with 7-T and the flop brings 6-T-T giving you a set with a 7 kicker. An opponent, however, is holding J-T and so has the same set but with a higher kicker.

To trap an opponent deliberately, you do a reverse-bluff with the intention of representing a strong hand as a weak one. Three conditions are necessary for this:

- The opposition must be good players who study and analyze their opponents' moves

- You need to be perceived as a player who can be expected to make the occasional risky play

- You need a top hand. Pre-flop it will be A-A or K-K. Post-flop, you should have at least a set or a straight

With these conditions met, you now make a much higher bet than is normal for you. The good players are likely to view this as an attempt to bluff them out of the pot, and thus put you on a weak hand. Being good players, they will do the correct thing and call (or even raise) your bet. By doing so they have allowed themselves to be trapped.

It is difficult to trap weak or timid players because they are fixated with their cards; they don't think about what the opposition may be up to. Making a big bet will just convince them that you have a big hand and they'll fold. It'll never occur to them that you may be bluffing.

Stack Size

The amount of cash you have on the table – your stack – is much more important in no-limit than it is in fixed-limit. To a certain degree, players who have a high stack in relation to their opponents have a "power" advantage (it's like having an army; a general with 10,000 troops is going to be much more powerful than one with 1,000).

High-stacked players command respect when they make a big bet and will often win pots unopposed, as opponents will be fearful of being faced with an all-in bet. Rather than risk a potentially expensive confrontation, they will back down. High-stacked players can try different stratagems and generally mix up their play. Basically, a high stack allows you to play optimum poker.

Contrast this with short-stacked players, who are inevitably under constant pressure. They will be called much more frequently because they do not have any "power". Even if they go all-in, it's not a threat to a high-stacked player. To avoid busting-out, they will often play negatively and, consequently, are likely to see their stack dwindle further.

Another big problem with being short-stacked is that when you do hit a monster hand, you won't be able to maximize the pay-off from it. You may have the great frustration of an opponent also hitting a good, but lesser, hand and being prepared to bet heavily on it. If you've only got $10, that's all you're going to get from your opponent – if you'd had $100, however ....

To limit the big advantage of a large stack, all poker rooms set a maximum buy-in amount for no-limit tables.

In no-limit your stack is often going to see-saw wildly. You must have an adequate amount in front of you in order to ride out the "downs", and, also, avoid the disadvantages of being short-stacked. For these reasons, it is a good idea to buy in for the maximum amount when joining a no-limit table. This starts you off with an immediate advantage over the short-stacked players.

Beware

Never sit down at a no-limit table with a small stack. Aggressive players will take advantage.

Beware

When playing no-limit poker be prepared to see your stack take wide swings in both directions. If you are of a nervous disposition, you might find this hard to handle.

Common No-Limit Mistakes

Not Bluffing (or Not Bluffing Enough)
This is one of the biggest mistakes. The bluff is a powerful weapon in no-limit and not using it is a major error.

Bluffing Too Much
By bluffing, you are telling the opposition that you have a good hand. However, good hands don't come along that often; bluff too much and your opponents simply won't believe you.

Overvaluing Pairs
This is very dangerous in no-limit. All too often, high pairs such as A-A and K-K will come up against a better hand. If the betting indicates your pair is beaten, just fold it.

Under-Betting
Quite simply, if you don't make large enough bets, your opponents will have no reason to fold their hands. This mistake will sting you big-time in the later stages of a game.

Overdoing the All-In Bet
A successful all-in move is the quickest and easiest way to win serious money at poker. The reverse is also true. You need to pick the times you do this carefully.

Not "Letting Go"
Continuing with a hand that's probably beaten. A typical example would be turning up 7-7 and seeing the flop, hoping for a set. If another 7 doesn't come, you should fold unless the pot odds are good. Many players will draw to the river in this situation, whatever the pot odds.

Playing the Cards Rather than the Players
An essential part of no-limit is knowing your opponents. Nearly every decision you make should be based on your observations of how they play. By doing this you will make far fewer mistakes. If you ignore this aspect and play only on the basis of what cards you have, you are going to miss out on many good opportunities, and, also, find yourself being manipulated by the opposition.

Beware

Of all the mistakes players make in no-limit poker, bluffing (either too much or too little) is probably the most common. If you can't get this right, you will find it difficult to win.

Hot tip

The other big mistake is concentrating more on your cards than you do on your opponents. If you can get a good "read" on how they play, you will often be able to win with weak hands that would have no chance in fixed-limit.

7 Online Poker

There is no doubt that online poker is here to stay as it offers many advantages over live poker rooms and casinos.

94 Live Versus Online

96 Online Poker Software

97 Cashing In

98 Bonuses

100 Pros & Cons of Online Poker

102 Three Top Poker Rooms

Live Versus Online

Online poker rooms are a completely different environment from their land-based counterparts. While the mechanics and strategy of the game are the same wherever you play, playing online does introduce some factors that won't be found in the traditional card room.

Hard Cash

Usually, in a live poker room you buy your chips with dollar bills. If you lose them, you have to hand over more dollar bills before you can get more chips. When you have no dollar bills left, you can't play any more. You can, of course, use a credit card to get more dollars, but by the time you've done this and gone back to the table, you've had time to think and may have second thoughts at the prospect of losing this as well.

In the online casino, however, there's no such thing as hard cash – the plastic card is king here – and all you see is numbers on a screen. When they have dwindled to zero, just click a few buttons and within a few seconds you're back in business. The sheer ease and speed with which you can deposit money in an online casino, plus the fact that you can't see or touch it, creates a mental disassociation that causes many people to lose sums of money online that they never would in a live casino.

Speed

Initially, the speed of online poker is bewildering. Because the games are so fast (50 or more hands an hour) you will be betting at least twice as much as you would in a live poker room in any given period. Bear this fact in mind when deciding what table limits to play; initially it might be prudent to play a lower limit than you would normally until you adjust to the speed of online play.

The element of speed also influences your actions at the table, for which you are allowed a specified length of time. Typically, this is around 20 to 30 seconds. If you fail to act within that time, the software automatically folds your hand. In other words, you have to think quickly.

Opponents

In an online poker room, you are completely isolated from your opponents; they could be aliens for all you know. This eliminates one of the most vital weapons in the good poker player's arsenal: being able to study opponents for any tell-tale signs of strength or weakness, and act accordingly. Many experienced players dislike playing online for this reason. For the inexperienced player, though, it's a definite advantage, and one less thing to have to think about.

Playing Options

Online poker rooms offer a huge range of tables at which to play. These range from the micro-limits at $0.01/0.02, up to the high-limits at $300/600. This gives you several advantages.

1) You are guaranteed to find a table that will suit your level of expertise. This is important for all but the very best players

2) There will always be a table available at which the action is at a suitable level for your bankroll. This is also very important. Betting at limits your bankroll can't sustain is a quick way to go broke

3) You will have a huge number of players against whom to play. For example, if a particular player is beating you consistently then you can simply move to another table. You will also be able to go "fishing" (looking for weak opponents)

4) You have several hundred poker rooms to choose from. If you don't like one for some reason, then take your action to a different one

Weighing it all up, the online poker room offers many advantages, particularly to the inexperienced player. Those brought up in the traditional bricks and mortar environment will find the inability to study opponents' body language a major disadvantage, though.

Hot tip

Because online poker doesn't allow players to study the opposition, the beginner will have a much better chance against those more used to live card rooms. In this respect it has a definite "leveling off" effect.

Online Poker Software

While all poker software packages do the same thing (enable you to play poker), some are definitely better than others. You need to consider the following:

Aesthetics

This is probably the least important consideration but as you may be spending hours looking at it, you may as well like what you see in terms of the layout and graphics.

Functionality

When you're sitting there with A-A, the last thing you need is for a buggy piece of software to stop responding or to freeze your PC. Unfortunately, this sort of thing does happen and can be extremely costly. This type of problem is much less likely with the well established poker sites that use tried-and-tested software. However, if you're trying out an unknown site, play at the micro-limit tables until you're satisfied on this point.

Software Options

Not all poker software provides the player with the same options and features. Examples are note-taking facilities, viewing options (resizable tables, game window customization, etc.), and downloading of hand histories to the player's PC. These are all worth having.

Another very useful feature to look out for is session statistics. As you play at the tables, statistics of all your actions are kept and are instantly available. This allows you to analyze your play in real-time (to a limited extent), or after your poker session. An example is shown below:

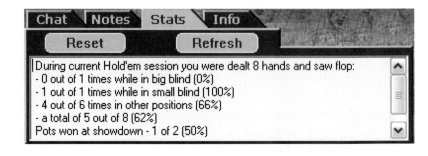

> **Hot tip**
>
> While not strictly a software issue, a site that drops your connection frequently due to problems with its servers is as bad as one that uses buggy software.

Cashing In

This is what it's all about – winning and then cashing in your chips. Sadly though, no poker room will ever give you your money with the same alacrity with which it takes it. While they will pay out eventually, the speed at which they do so varies considerably. This issue is one of the biggest grouches players have with online poker sites.

Some sites have better cash-out procedures than others. The best ones handle your cash-out request promptly. This usually means a 1-3 day wait on your first cash-out request while they do some anti-fraud checks. Subsequent withdrawals will usually be handled within 24 hours. Once the withdrawal has been approved, some additional time may be required depending on the cash-out method. Neteller takes only a few seconds, an electronic funds transfer two or three days, a mailed bank draft a week or more.

So how can you, the player, tell which poker rooms have a quick cash-out policy and which don't? Most will tell you their policy when you click the software's Withdrawal option. However, relying on this is akin to believing a politician's promises; you really need something more concrete.

One way is to deposit the minimum amount, immediately cash it out and see how long it takes to reappear in your account. However, this doesn't cover the possibility that the site will deliberately drag its heels on large withdrawals only – and some do. (Usually, in this situation, they will cite the need for security and may even demand to see proof of identity. If you live in Poland and the site is based in Belize, you can envisage the problems you may have.)

So, the Internet is where you go. Here you will get feedback on all casinos and poker rooms. If you can't find much information in general on the site in question, be immediately suspicious. Also, check the websites of the various gaming watchdogs and take a look at their lists of blacklisted casinos and poker rooms. Poker user forums are another good source of information.

| Hot tip | |

Five sites with good reputations for prompt handling of cash-outs are: Poker Stars, Party Poker, Ladbrokes, Ultimate Bet and Paradise Poker.

Bonuses

Online poker sites all want a slice of your cash. While live poker rooms and casinos offer players free meals, drinks, and rooms as incentives, online poker rooms have only one thing to give you – hard cash. However, there are catches involved. So let's take a look at what's on offer (and the catches).

Sign-Up Bonuses

To lure players into their sites, poker rooms offer a sign-up bonus. These vary according to the site, but usually they will be up to a maximum of $500 depending on the size of the initial deposit. At Party Poker, for example, the maximum is $500 and to qualify for it you must deposit $500.

This all sounds wonderful but, unfortunately, there is a snag as you'll discover if you try to cash-out your bonus immediately – the poker room won't let you. To be able to claim your bonus, you must first "earn it", and this involves staking a specified amount of cash, or playing a specified number of raked hands. This gives the poker room an opportunity to get some (if not all) of the bonus back. For example, one of them demands that you wager 20 times the bonus amount ($10,000 to get the maximum bonus of $500). Some also specify a time limit, whereby you will need to play a certain number of raked hands within a specified period.

Loyalty Bonuses

Having got your business, the poker rooms want to keep it; they don't want you taking your money elsewhere. To this end, they offer loyalty bonuses. The more you wager and play with a poker room, the higher your loyalty rating will be. Some pay on-going bonuses according to the amounts you deposit. Others give bonuses on a weekly or monthly basis.

A popular type of loyalty bonus currently in vogue is known as "cashback" or "rakeback". This is basically a percentage of the rake you have paid in a given period (usually one month), which is then returned to you in the form of a bonus.

Beware

If a particular site's sign-up bonus gets your attention, be sure to read the small print before giving them your money. Some sites make it very difficult to actually earn the bonus.

Hot tip

Good loyalty bonuses are worth far more than sign-up bonuses. In the long term, they will earn you much more money.

Other Bonuses

There are any number of these, and as with the loyalty bonuses, they can be well worth looking out for. A typical example here is the happy hour bonus. Make a deposit between, say, 10:00pm and midnight, and you'll receive a free $10 chip.

Another method of rewarding players is by awarding them points. This can be based on numerous factors, such as number of hands played, playing at a certain limit, depositing certain amounts, etc. These points can be converted into cash or used as buy-ins for tournaments.

High rollers are rewarded for staking large sums. These bonuses range from $500 to $5000.

Most poker rooms award jackpots for hitting a royal flush (the best poker hand possible), and bad-beats (the best losing hand). These jackpots are usually progressive and increase by a certain amount each day until a lucky player qualifies.

Bonus Players

These are players who play only for the sign-up bonuses. As soon as they've earned one, they cash it in and move on to another site.

This is a very common practice of which the casinos and poker rooms are well aware. While it's perfectly legal and above board, needless to say they are not enamoured with it.

If you decide to do this yourself, be aware that there is a blacklist circulating around the sites containing the names of known bonus players. If you happen to be on this list, you will find that many sites will simply refuse to pay you the bonus.

Obviously, you will be able to do it a number of times before they catch on to you, but if you overdo it, you will eventually find yourself blacklisted.

Hot tip

The bonus details described on these pages were correct at the time of going to press. However, they may well have changed by the time you are reading this. Our purpose here is just to give you an idea of what's on offer.

66

Beware

If you play only for bonuses, the poker rooms will soon realize what you're up to and put a stop to it.

Pros & Cons of Online Poker

Accessibility

Probably the biggest plus for online poker, particularly for the senior citizen and those who simply can't get out and about for whatever reason, is the fact that it can be played in your own home.

Furthermore, it is available 24 hours a day so should you find yourself unable to sleep in the early hours for example, you can get up and play a few hands.

Choice

Go into a typical casino and you will see a few Roulette and Blackjack tables, maybe a craps table, loads of slot machines, and one or two poker tables – not much choice for the poker player. Furthermore, what choice there is may well be at higher limits than you are comfortable with.

In an online poker room on the other hand, you will have dozens, if not hundreds, of tables to choose from, not to mention other types of poker such as Omaha and Stud. The advantages this offers are numerous: for example, every limit is catered for so you will have no trouble finding a table that you can afford to play at. Also, the sheer number of tables means that you can change tables at will without having to wait ages for a seat, as you may well have to in a live poker room. If your luck is out at one table, or the general style of play doesn't suit you, simply move to a different one.

Playing Aids

Online poker software offers many features that aren't available to players in live poker rooms.

It does the counting for you – you can see at a glance exactly how much you have in your stack, plus the stacks of your opponents. You don't need to count what's in the pot or how much you need to call a bet because the software tells you.

Another great aid is that the software tells you what your best hand is. For example, in a live game it can be easy to miss the fact that you've hit a straight.

Hot tip

Even on Christmas Day, you will find people playing poker online.

Hot tip

Should you find it helps your game, you can use whatever hardware or software aids you like.

100

...cont'd

With online software you always know what you have. This can be particularly important for beginners.

Downloadable histories of all the hands you've played, the ability to search for specific players, being able to quickly make notes about every player, etc., are just some of the others.

Anonymity

Making a silly mistake in an online poker room is not as embarrassing as it would be in a live poker room, as no one can see you. Also, for the beginner, live poker can be an intimidating experience, initially.

Multi-Tabling

One of the greatest boons of online poker, especially for serious players, is the ability to play several tables at once. Good players can win much more in a given period playing online due to this feature. Bad players, however, can lose much more, which of course is compounded by the fact that many more hands are played per hour online.

There are, of course, drawbacks to Internet poker. For good players who habitually study their opponents for tells, the anonymity of online play removes an important weapon from their arsenal.

There is also the issue of personal interaction. Many players in live poker rooms enjoy the friendly banter at the table. There is much less of this in the online poker room.

The ease of access, which is in many ways a plus, can be a minus if you find that it is hard for you to resist the lure of a game. Since games are always available from your home or office computer, you might find it too difficult to restrain yourself from playing poker more than you know you should.

Hot tip

Software is available (see page 165) that can analyze your hand histories, and give you an amazing range of statistics. This is very useful in plugging leaks in your game.

101

Three Top Poker Rooms

Currently, three top online poker rooms are Ladbrokes Poker, Poker Stars and Party Poker. Play at any of these sites and you will have a good and trouble-free online poker experience.

Ladbrokes Poker
Operated by a well established bookmaker in the UK, Ladbrokes Poker is very popular with European players.

The games offered are Texas Hold'em, Omaha, Omaha Hi-Lo, Seven-Card Stud, Five-Card Draw and Five-Card Stud.

Limits range from the micro at $0.01/0.02 up to $25/50 plus.

Real-money player statistics as of June 2009 show 1400 ring-game players and 5000 tournament players at peak hours.

The site offers a maximum $500 sign-up bonus, plus numerous other bonuses and promotions. The best of these is the rakeback bonus, which returns up to 25% of the amount of rake payed each month.

The site's server is fast and reliable and the software offers all the usual features, such as multi-tabling, resizable tables, etc.

Hot tip

The majority of players on Ladbrokes are European, and include many Scandinavian and British players.

Hot tip

Ladbrokes also offers an option that enables you to instantly replay any hand. This is very useful for identifying (and eliminating) mistakes.

...cont'd

Poker Stars

Poker Stars is the largest online poker room in the world and offers a huge number of poker variants. These include: Texas Hold'em, Omaha and Seven-Card Stud in all versions, H.O.R.S.E, H.O.S.E, 2-7 Triple Draw, Five-Card Draw, Razz, 2-7 Single Draw Lowball, Badugi, 8-Game, Mixed Hold'em and Mixed Omaha Hi/Lo.

Game limits are from $0.01/0.02 to a maximum of $1000/2000.

Real-money player statistics as of June 2009 show 22,500 ring-game players at peak hours and 155,000 tournament players at peak hours. The latter figure shows quite clearly that you if enjoy playing tournaments, Poker Stars is, without question, the site for you. A huge range is available, in all types, sizes and limits.

The software is excellent and offers many options to customize it to suit your preferences.

The sign-up bonus is not as generous as most, being a mere $50.

Don't forget

For choice of tables, Poker Stars cannot be beaten, especially if you play tournaments.

Hot tip

The sign-up bonus at this site is less than stellar.

...cont'd

Party Poker

Party Poker is the second biggest online poker site. It is well known for running many satellites and special events, including the famous Party Poker Million.

Games on offer here include all variations of Texas Hold'em, Omaha, Omaha Hi-Lo, Seven-Card Stud and Seven-Card Stud Hi-Lo.

Limits are $0.02/0.04 up to $250/500.

Real-money player statistics as of June 2009 show 9500 ring-game players and 60,000 tournament players during peak hours.

A major software redesign in Sept 2008 has added a lot of new features, including better graphics, a quick-seat feature, a live action preview, customized player images and several enhanced multi-tabling options.

Party Poker offers a maximum sign-up bonus of $500 for new players. There are also many other bonuses and promotions.

Don't forget

Party Poker offers a nice sign-up bonus to a maximum of $500.

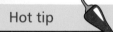

Hot tip

Party Poker's loyalty bonus takes the form of party points, which can be redeemed in various ways.

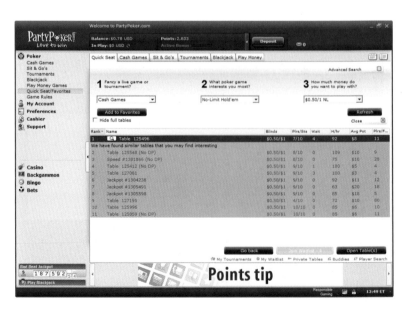

8 Omaha

Now we look at other poker games, starting with Omaha and Omaha Hi/Lo. Start hand requirements and strategies for all stages of these games are explained with the aid of sample hands.

106 Introduction

108 Evaluating Your Start Cards

110 Playable Start Cards

115 Low-Hand Qualification

116 Pre-Flop Strategy

117 Reading the Board

118 Counterfeiting

119 Playing the Flop

122 The Turn and the River

124 Common Omaha Mistakes

Introduction

Next to Texas Hold'em, Omaha is the most popular version of poker. There are two variations of this game: Omaha High and Omaha Hi/Lo (also known as Omaha Eight). Both types are available in the majority of poker rooms, both online and live.

The mechanics of Omaha are very similar to Texas Hold'em – start cards, four betting rounds, community cards and the blinds. However, there are two major differences, which make the dynamics of Omaha completely different.

These are:

1)   Players are dealt four start cards instead of two

2)   When making a hand, players can only use two of their start cards. The other two are discarded

The fact that there are four start cards makes the starting hand requirements considerably different to those in Texas Hold'em. This is the first thing that Omaha beginners will have to learn. The main effect is that hand values are considerably lower than in Hold'em. With two extra cards, monster hands like full houses and quads are much more likely to be seen. Hands that are excellent in Hold'em (straights, flushes, and sets) are regularly beaten in Omaha.

The requirement that a hand must consist of two of the player's start cards and three of the community cards may seem, on the face of it, to be a fairly simple concept to understand. It is, however, quite confusing initially, and takes some time to grasp. Beginners often think they have hit a good hand when, in fact, they have nothing (even pros misread Omaha hands occasionally).

Omaha Hi/Lo introduces another element: the concept of two winning hands, the highest hand winning half the pot and the lowest hand winning the other half. Sometimes, a hand is both the highest and the lowest and scoops the entire pot.

Hot tip

It is important that you are aware of the fact that good hands in Texas Hold'em are marginal hands in Omaha.

Hot tip

With nine cards available, it is much more common for players to hit a good hand in Omaha. This in turn leads to more betting (thus, bigger pots) and general action. This makes Omaha a more exciting game than Texas Hold'em.

This is the game that we're going to concentrate on in this chapter.

Although it's confusing initially, once you've got to grips with it you'll find that Omaha is actually a simpler and more straightforward game than Texas Hold'em. It is also generally considered to be the easiest of the online poker games to win at.

The reason for this is that a high degree of skill is not required. The differential between good and bad players is much less than in Texas Hold'em for this reason. A good strategy, and the discipline to stick to it, will be enough to beat most players, especially at the lower limits.

Most players graduate to Omaha from Texas Hold'em and, initially, assume that what was good there will also be good in Omaha. For example, they will play a pair of aces in the same way they would in Hold'em, not realizing that in Omaha this hand has little chance of winning a pot by itself. Also, Omaha is particularly unforgiving on the two fundamental mistakes that most players make – playing bad start cards, and not knowing when to fold.

Omaha is a drawing game; players are looking to hit a five-card hand, which means a straight or higher. Pairs, two-pairs, and even sets (to a lesser degree) are not good hands at all. With four start cards, most players will be on a draw of some kind, and usually at least one or two will bet through to the river. For this reason, tactical skills, such as bluffing, check-raising, and positional play, which are so important in Texas Hold'em, lose much of their effectiveness.

The basis of playing Omaha to win is start card selection. Remember, this game is all about hitting big five-card hands, which means drawing plenty of cards. To do this profitably, you need start cards that give you several possibilities of hitting that big hand.

Hot tip

On average, a good player will win 50% more in any given hour in Omaha than in Texas Hold'em.

107

Evaluating Your Start Cards

To win at Omaha, you will need very strong hands. At the minimum, you should be looking to make a straight. Even sets, which are a powerful hand in Texas Hold'em, are often beaten.

The first thing we'll look at is how to evaluate your start cards. While you have four of these, remember that you can only use *two* of them. We'll do this with some examples:

This looks like a wonderful hand; alas, it's not. Actually, it's a trash hand. Why? Because although you've got four queens, the rules state that you can only use two of them. So all you've actually got is two queens. Furthermore, as the other two queens are out, there is no way to make a set, or quads. Also, you have no flush or straight draws. Fold it; you'll only lose money with this hand.

108

This also looks like a wonderful hand and, indeed, it is. You've got two top pairs (although you can only use one of them), a flush draw in both hearts and diamonds, two straight flush draws, plus a chance of quads or a full house.

A final example:

Omaha start cards should offer at least two different ways of hitting a strong hand. If they don't, they are not worth playing.

This is a good hand. While you don't have quad or full house possibilities, you have a flush draw in both hearts and spades, and three straight draws (8-9, 9-T, and T-J). This hand you will definitely play.

Omaha Hi/Lo introduces another variable – the split pot. Here, players have two targets – the highest hand, which takes half the pot, and the lowest hand, which takes the other half.

The lowest hand must include five cards (two from the player's hand and three from the community cards) between an ace and an eight. For example, 2-4-5-7-8. If no player manages to make a low card hand then the entire pot is won by the highest hand. It is also possible for a player to win both hi and lo pots. For example, an A-2-3-4-5 straight.

Determining the strength of a low-hand can be confusing, so we'll explain this a bit more (also, see the margin note). The best possible complete hand is A-2-3-4-5. The second best hand is A-2-3-4-6. The third best is A-2-3-4-7, and so on. The worst hand is 4-5-6-7-8.

It is also possible for a player to have both the lowest and the highest hand, and thus "scoop" the entire pot. An example would be: Ah-2h-3h-5h-6h. Here, the hand gives the nut flush for the high-hand and, also, a very good low-hand.

Ideally then, you want a hand that will be both the highest and the lowest. We'll take a look now at the start cards that you should be playing in Omaha Hi/Lo, and the ones you should be folding.

Hot tip

You need to be aware that while an ace is the best low card you can hold, it's not the determining factor in how good your low-hand is. It is, in fact, the least significant card. When evaluating the strength of a low-hand, you work down from the highest card.

For example: player A has 8-7-5-3-2 and player B has 8-7-5-4-A. You might think that player B has the best hand because of the ace. In fact, it's player A.

Working downwards, the first three cards (8-7-5) are common to both players. The deciding cards are the fourth – player A's 3 is lower than player B's 4.

Playable Start Cards

When your start cards are dealt, you have three things to consider:

1)   Will they make a high-hand?

2)   Will they make a low-hand?

3)   Will they make a high-hand and, also, a low-hand?

High-Hand Start Cards

Here you are looking for cards that will give you as many ways to make a hand as possible. You need to remember the following:

● Pairs, and two pairs, are not good hands in Omaha. Cards that are unlikely to make better hands than these should be folded

● A straight is often the *minimum* hand needed to win

● Your hand should contain at least one (preferably two) high suited connectors

The best possible hand is A-A-K-K double-suited, as shown below.

The best of the rest is any four-card combination between an ace and a ten. For example, Q-J-A-A, K-T-T-A, K-K-A-T, etc. If two of the cards are connected, so much the better; this increases the chances of a straight. If the cards are suited then you have a flush draw. These hands you will play in any position.

Hot tip

Forget the hand values you learned in Texas Hold'em. In Omaha, the lowest hand you can bet on with any degree of confidence is a straight, and even with this you need to be wary.

Hot tip

The ideal high-hand will be four high cards, connected and double-suited.

Dangerous High-Hand Start Cards

Low cards, generally, should not be played. If you make a hand, it is going to be a low-card one, and you will end up with the second best hand time after time.

The following are the types of hand you should not play:

- Middle and low card flush and straight draws
- Middle and low pairs
- One high pair with nothing else

To illustrate the dangers of playing these hands, we'll look at a couple of typical examples:

These cards offer several straight draws and one flush draw. Say the flop brings 8-T-J. This gives you a jack high straight, which you will no doubt consider to be a good hand. An opponent who is holding 8-9-Q-Q, though, will have a queen high straight. Your hand was good but it wasn't the nuts (or even close to it). Playing these low and middle card draws will cost you dearly.

Here you hold two fours and, also, a low flush draw. You bet and the flop brings As-4s-9c, giving you a set, and an outside chance of a flush. All but one of your opponents fold.

Beware

Playing low and middle ranked start cards is a recipe for disaster in Omaha.

...cont'd

You have a reasonable hand (the set), and also have a chance of a flush. Furthermore, the board doesn't look too threatening. With only one opponent to beat, you think you have a very good chance of winning. You bet and your opponent calls the bet.

The turn card brings the seven of clubs. Needing one more club for your flush and with a set as a backup, you bet. Your opponent calls and the river card brings the queen of clubs giving you the flush. You bet the hand out, the showdown comes, and your opponent turns up 7s-7h-Kc-5c. The other player not only had a higher set, but also hit a higher flush.

The lesson in all this? You played a low pair that was never going to lead to a nut hand. Unfortunately, you hit a reasonable hand (the set) that enticed you to continue playing. This gave you a chance to turn the reasonable hand into a good hand (the low flush). You hit this and, on the strength of it, bet the hand out.

You trapped yourself; once you got involved with these cards, you couldn't get out. Don't forget, low and middle pairs rarely result in a hand good enough to win.

Low-Hand Start Cards

As we have already noted, the best possible complete low-hand is five cards of consecutive rank from an ace to a five, i.e. A-2-3-4-5. The worst possible hand is 4-5-6-7-8.

Pairs, sets, straights, flushes, quads and full houses have no relevance with regard to low-hands. All that counts is that you have five *different* ranks between an ace and an eight. Cards above eight do not qualify. This makes evaluating your start cards extremely straightforward – you need just two cards between an ace and an eight, the lower the better. The ideal hand, therefore, will contain an ace and a two. An ace and a three is not so good, an ace and a four even less so, and so on.

You also have another factor to consider.

Don't forget

Be absolutely clear on this, low-hands must contain five cards between an ace and an eight. Also, you can't use two cards of the same rank (see page 115).

Ideally, you want to win the high-hand as well. This will enable you to scoop the entire pot, instead of just half of it. This complicates things; all of a sudden, sets, straights, flushes, etc., are back in the equation. Consider the following:

As regards the low-hand, you have an ace and a four; the best card and a reasonable card. However, you have absolutely nothing with which to make a high-hand – no pairs, no straight draw, no flush draw. Compare this with the example below:

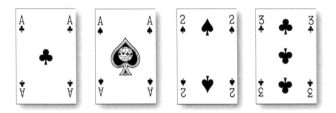

Here, you have an ace and a two, which are the best possible cards for a low-hand. For the high-hand, you have a pair of aces (possible set, quads, and full house), two flush draws and a straight draw. Furthermore, if any of these hands hit, they will be the nuts. Let's see another type of hand:

These cards give you a chance of a good high-hand (J-J) or a good low-hand (2-3) but not both.

Hot tip

If you get confused with the examples on this page, remember the following two rules:

You can use only two of your start cards.

You can use the same two start cards for both the low-hand and the high-hand.

113

…cont'd

Hot tip

The table here makes it clear that you should be playing only very high cards, very low cards, or combinations of the two.

Don't forget

High-hand start cards should include at least two suited cards to give the chance of a flush.

Below, are the recommended start cards for Omaha Hi/Lo:

Top Hands
A-A-2-2, A-A-2-3, A-A-2-x, A-A-3-x, A-2-3-x, A-2-K-K, A-2-Q-Q, A-3-4-5, A-3-4-6, A-3-5-6, A-2-K-J, 2-3-Q-Q, 2-3-K-K, A-3-K-K, A-3-Q-Q, A-2-K-Q, A-A-K-K, A-A-Q-Q
Good Hands
A-2-x-x, 2-3-4-x, A-K-Q-J, K-Q-J-T, K-Q-J-9, A-K-Q-T, K-K-J-J, K-K-2-4, Q-J-T-9, A-A-x-x, K-K-Q-Q, A-3-x-x, K-K-T-T
A – Ace, K – King, Q – Queen, J – Jack, T – Ten, 9 to 2 – card value, x – any card

The important things to remember are:

High-Hand

The hand must contain four cards, ten or above. This gives you a good chance of hitting at least a high straight. If you play lower cards, you are going to end up hitting the second-best hand time after time.

At least two of the cards should be suited to give the chance of a flush.

Hands containing four cards of the same rank, e.g. J-J-J-J must be folded, as they offer nothing better than a pair.

Low-Hand

The hand must contain two cards between an ace and a three. If you play cards higher than these, you will hit second-best hands far too often.

Suited and connected cards are important only with regard to the high-hand. They add nothing in terms of value to the low-hand.

If you have a pair, eight or lower, you will not be able to make a low-hand unless you have another low card of a different rank (see page 115).

Low-Hand Qualification

We have already seen that to qualify as a low-hand, the hand must contain five cards, eight or lower. However, there are two other conditions that confuse many people initially.

1) Sets, straights, flushes, quads, etc., do not count towards the strength of a low-hand

2) You can use only one card of a particular rank – paired cards don't count twice

Don't forget

Pairs, two-pairs, sets, straights, flushes, full houses and quads only count toward the high-hand. For the low-hand, they have no relevance.

For example, you have the Ac-4c in your hand and the board shows the 6c-7c-8c, as shown above. Thus, you have a club flush. The flush does not count towards your low-hand, though; your low-hand is just A-4-6-7-8. An opponent holding A-3-6-7-8 with no flush has a better low-hand. However, it does count towards your high-hand. The same applies to straights. If you have 4-5-6-7-8, an opponent holding A-2-3-7-8 will beat you for the low-hand. Your straight will count towards your high-hand, though.

Beware

Pairs do not count twice towards a low-hand. Remember this. Otherwise, you will think you have a qualified low-hand when, in fact, you don't.

You're holding a five and a six, and the board has three cards below nine. Thus, you may think you have a low-hand: 3-3-5-6-8. Unfortunately, though, you don't. This is because you can only use a card of a particular rank once. In the example above, only one of the threes counts towards your hand. All you've actually got is 3-5-6-8, which is not a hand at all.

Pre-Flop Strategy

Hot tip

Another exception to the rule of not raising pre-flop is if the best hand you are likely to make is a straight. In this case, you will need to force out the flush draws. It must be said, though, that if a straight is your best prospect, you would probably be better off folding the hand.

Hot tip

It can be difficult to weigh up the value of a low-hand. Try thinking of it like this: a two is the equivalent of a king, a three the equivalent of a queen, a four the equivalent of a jack, and so on.

The strategy outlined here is based on playing the start cards recommended on page 114. If you stick to these, you will usually be drawing to nut hands, or very close to them. Thus, if you hit your hand, it will usually take the pot.

As a general rule, with top hands you should not raise the pot pre-flop. If you do, you risk your opponents folding as they are going to know you have a good hand. By just calling, you won't give them any warning. This will encourage them to stay in the game. Notice that this is completely contrary to Texas Hold'em strategy. There, you play top start cards like A-A aggressively to limit the competition because they are so vulnerable to drawing hands post-flop. In Omaha, you want the opposition to remain in the game because if you hit your hand it's going to win.

Another advantage of not raising pre-flop is that if the flop misses you completely, you can then fold without having lost too much money. The exception to this is if you are on the button (last to act). The opposition will have already put money in the pot, and thus will be less inclined to fold to a raise. By raising in this position only, you will build the pot, and at the same time cause fewer opponents to fold than would otherwise be the case.

If you play cards that are not likely to hit a nut hand (those in the Good Hands category in the table on page 114), then raising pre-flop to drive out some of the competition is not a bad move. Basically, you should play these hands as you would a pair of aces or kings in Texas Hold'em. Never forget: Omaha is a game of nut hands. If you don't have the best possible hand of any type, you are going to get beaten frequently unless you can limit the competition.

As a final note, be very wary of betting heavily on a low-hand if it doesn't contain an ace. At a ten-seat table, 40 cards will be dealt to the players, and five will be dealt as community cards. That leaves only seven cards not in play. If you don't have an ace, someone else almost certainly will.

Reading the Board

Before we get into post-flop strategy, there are two things that you must be clear on. The first is that you know how to read the board in relation to your start cards. Remember, you can only use three of the community cards – no more, no less, just *three*. The hand is completed by *two* of your start cards. Let's see a couple of examples:

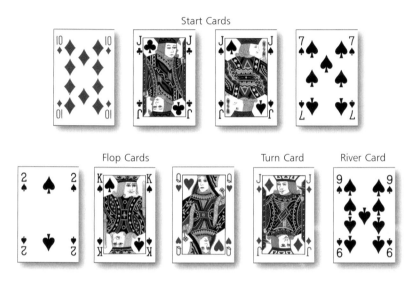

Here you have several options: a straight, a set of jacks and a king high spade flush. Your best hand is the flush.

Hot tip

It is absolutely essential that you can read the board quickly without making a mistake. As you can see from the examples on this page, with nine cards to look at, and the requirement that you use two of your start cards and three from the board, it isn't easy.

...cont'd

You must have something really good here: queen quads? A full house (queens full of kings)? A king high flush? Sadly, not. A set of queens with a king kicker is the best you can muster. If these examples aren't obvious to you then get a pack of cards, deal some hands and practice reading them.

Counterfeiting

The second thing you need to know about is counterfeiting and the effect it can have on a low-hand. Counterfeiting occurs when one of your low-hand start cards is matched by one falling on the board. The board card nullifies or "counterfeits" the card in your hand, and effectively weakens it. Whereas before you may have had the best hand, you may now find yourself holding the second-best hand.

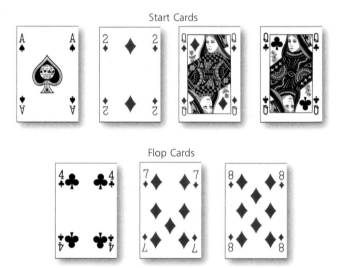

You have a low-hand of A-2-4-7-8. However, the turn card brings another 2. Note that this doesn't change your hand: you still have A-2-4-7-8. However, an opponent holding A-3-9-9 will now have A-2-3-4-7, whereas before the turn it was A-3-4-7-8 (worse than yours). Your hand is now beaten.

Hot tip

Another way to look at counterfeiting is in high-hand terms. For example, you are holding J-T and the flop is 9-8-7 giving you the nut straight. The turn card, however, is a T. Now, an opponent holding J-Q will have a 8-9-T-J-Q straight, which beats your 7-8-9-T-J. The T falling on the turn counterfeited the T in your hand.

Beware

Because of the danger of having the best hand counterfeited, be very wary when a card falls on the board and matches one in your low-hand, particularly if it's an ace or a two.

Playing the Flop

At the flop stage, always be aware of the following:

- Pairs and two-pairs rarely win. Even sets often end up as second- or third-best hands

- Whenever there is a pair on the board, there is a strong possibility that someone has a full house

- A straight is often the minimum hand needed to win the high-hand

- You should always be looking to hit the nuts in whatever type of hand you are trying to make

- Don't bank on being able to out-play the opposition. Tactics play a lesser role in Omaha

If you bear the above in mind, your decisions will usually be correct. You won't be throwing away the money that many other players do by drawing to hands that are never going to win even if they hit them.

We'll start with two examples of hands you should fold:

119

Don't forget

In Omaha, you should always be looking to hit a five-card hand (straights, flushes or full houses). While two-pairs do take some pots, they don't do it often enough to make these hands worth playing.

Hot tip

Whenever the board is paired, full houses become a real possibility. However, in the example here, even if the board hadn't been paired, you would still have to consider folding because of the flush possibility. At best, you would call and see what the turn card was.

Start Cards

 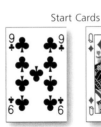  

Flop Cards

...cont'd

There is a case to be made for playing this hand. You have Q-Q and several straight draws. Furthermore, they are all high, so if you hit one it's going to be close to the nuts. However, the board is paired (J-J), and with four start cards it's almost certain that an opponent has a pair in his or her start cards, and thus is very close to a full house. Plus, there are two hearts on the board so a flush is also a very strong possibility. Even if you hit your straight, there are too many ways it can be beaten to justify the attempt.

Start Cards

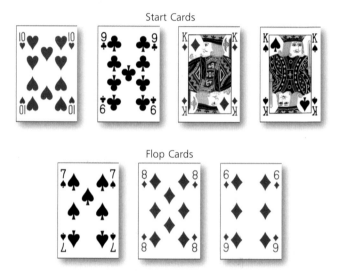

Flop Cards

Here, you've flopped a middle straight – 6-7-8-9-T. It's also a high-end straight, and you will probably play it to the end. However, an opponent holding J-T only needs a 9 to complete a higher straight. You may think this to be unlikely, but remember, there are two cards still to come and your opponents have four start cards to choose from. It is, in fact, extremely likely.

Even so, it might be worth playing this hand it if weren't for one thing: the lack of a low-hand. You have no cards below a 9, which means you have no way to make a low-hand, and so can only win half the pot. The risk outweighs the reward. This hand you should probably fold. At best, you would call, but fold to a raise.

Beware

When deciding whether to play a marginal hand that can win only one end of the pot, remember that even if it wins, you will only get half the money that's in the pot.

Furthermore, if an opponent has the same hand, that end of the pot will be split, in which case you will get only a quarter of it.

In Omaha, this is known as being "three-quartered". Very often, it won't be worth playing the hand for this reason.

Now, we'll look at a couple of situations where you should raise.

Start Cards

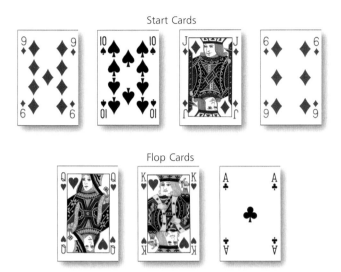

Flop Cards

You have flopped a nut straight (T-J-Q-K-A). The problem, though, is that there are two hearts on the board. If either the turn or the river brings another heart then your straight is in danger of being trumped by a flush. If the turn and river cards are both hearts then your straight will almost certainly be beaten. Remember, the chance of a flush turning up is much greater than in Texas Hold'em.

So you raise. If everyone folds, you'll win a small pot. Better that, though, than losing a big one. If they don't fold, and a heart doesn't come, you've built the pot for your straight.

Let's say you have a A-3-5-6-8 low-hand, which is good but not wonderful. You also have a J-J high-hand, but anyone holding an A, K or Q can beat this on the turn or river.

So you need to do two things here: limit the competition, and also find out if anyone has better cards. The only way to do this is to raise the pot. If enough of the opposition fold, it's worth paying to see the turn card. However, if you are re-raised then you are probably beaten already, and should either fold, or just call.

Hot tip

Playing the flop in Omaha can be somewhat mechanical as everyone is trying to hit the same types of hand – straights, flushes and full houses. Often, it comes down to seeing whose hand is closest to the nuts.

The Turn and the River

Hot tip

If the pot is big and you have a chance to scoop it by winning both the high- and low-hands, it is usually worth paying to see the river card (see margin note below).

If you've already hit your hand, it should be the nuts, or very close to it (assuming you're playing the correct start cards). Play the cards in the way most likely to get your opponents' money in the pot.

If you haven't, however, you need to consider how much of the pot you are likely to win if you manage to make the hand on the turn or the river. For example:

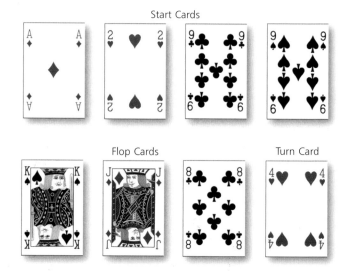

Start Cards

Flop Cards   Turn Card

Hot tip

As an illustration of why scooping the pot is so important, consider the following:

If the final pot is $100 and you have contributed $25, by winning half of it ($50) your profit is $25. However, if you scoop the entire pot ($100) your profit is $75.

In the first instance you are getting even money on your bet, and in the second, you are getting odds of 3:1.

You need the river card to be a 3, 5, 6 or 7 to complete a low-hand. Your pair of nines has little chance of taking the high-hand. Unless the pot is very big, it's not worth paying another bet to try and win half the money. Fold the hand and wait for a better opportunity.

If you have one half of the pot covered with a very good hand (high or low), you should try and take the other half as well. For example:

In the hand shown on the next page, you've got the nut flush for the high-hand, but no low-hand. Most players would slow-play in this situation. However, if you raise, you may get opponents with a low-hand draw to fold. You would then win the entire pot and get a bigger pay-off than you may otherwise have done.

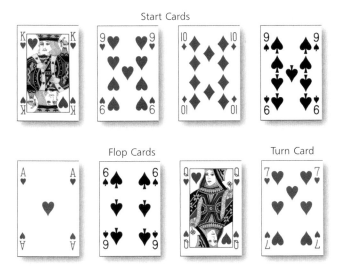

Start Cards

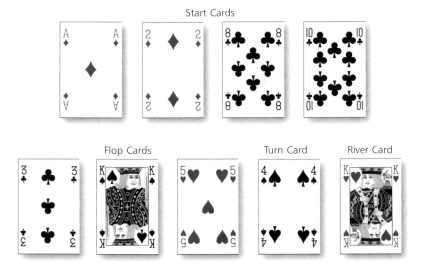

Slow-playing should only be done when you are certain that you cannot be beaten, and there's no realistic prospect of taking the other half of the pot by raising. For example:

123

You've got the best possible low-hand, but no high-hand. With K-K on the board, it is quite likely that someone has a set, if not a full house. You're not going to bluff anyone out of those hands by raising. So, try and maximize the pay-off from your low-hand by calling and checking to keep as many opponents in the game as possible.

Common Omaha Mistakes

Playing Poor Start Cards

With nine cards with which to make a hand, the possibility of several good hands being hit in any one game is extremely likely. This fact makes sensible start-card selection more critical than in any other form of poker. Low-hands, in particular, should only be played if they include A-2, A-3 or 2-3.

Misreading Hands

This is a very easy (and costly) mistake to make in Omaha Hi/Lo. The requirement that: a) all hands must consist of two start cards and three board cards, and b) that low-hands must contain five cards, eight or lower, demands a high level of concentration. This is definitely not a game to play if you are tired or subject to outside distractions.

Overvaluing Hands

With the increased opportunity to hit a really good hand, hands such as high pairs, two-pairs and sets should be played cautiously. By this we don't mean timidly, but rather that you be conscious of the fact that they are easily beaten.

Not Taking Note of a Paired Board

Whenever the board is paired, there is a real danger of an opponent hitting either quads or a full house. In these situations, straights and flushes can be dangerous hands to be holding. If a pair falling on the board is followed by heavy betting action, folding is usually the sensible option.

Forgetting the Nuts Rule

In Omaha it is quite common to see a flush or straight beaten by a better flush or straight. Therefore, only play a drawing hand if it will be the nuts if you hit it.

Raising Pre-Flop With Top Hands

As a general rule you should do the opposite with top hands than you would in Texas Hold'em. Instead of raising to force out the competition, you should slow-play to keep as many opponents in as possible. It's at the turn and river stages that you start raising.

9 Seven-Card Stud

Seven-Card Stud is a very strategic game that requires a great deal more skill than do Texas Hold'em and Omaha. This chapter gives you the low-down on this game and shows how to win.

126 Seven-Card Stud – the Rules

128 Factors Specific to Seven-Card Stud

130 Start Cards

131 Playing Pairs

134 Playing Sets

137 Playing Two Pairs

139 Playing Flush Draws

141 Playing Straight Draws

143 Playing Killer Hands

Seven-Card Stud – The Rules

Until the rise of Texas Hold'em, Seven-Card Stud was, for many years, the poker game of choice for most people, not only in the USA but in many other countries, Europe in particular.

To play Seven-Card Stud successfully, you need a high degree of skill, endless patience, good observation, and an extremely good memory. For these reasons, it is a difficult game to master.

An important point to note is that the betting in Seven-Card Stud is usually fixed or spread. If it's fixed, there is a small ante and a big ante – $2.00/4.00, for example. If it's spread, the house sets a range – say, $2.00 to $10.00, and players can bet or raise in increments of any figure within that range. Furthermore, the number of raises is usually capped at three.

No-limit versions are available but these are difficult to find.

The game is played as follows:

The Ante
Before the cards are dealt, each player places an "ante" on the table. Usually, this is equal to one quarter of the game's lower limit. For example, if the game is being played at a $1.00/2.00 table, it will be $0.25. The ante is the equivalent of the blinds in Texas Hold'em and serves the same purpose.

Third Street
First, all the antes are raked to the middle of the table. Then, beginning with the player to the left of the dealer button, each player is dealt two face-down cards and one face-up card (known as the door-card).

This is the first betting round and it is initiated by the player holding the lowest door-card. The first bet is known as the "bring-in" and is usually set at half the lower table limit. For example, at a $2.00/4.00 table, the first player must make a bet of at least $1. Any raises in this round can only be in increments of the lower limit.

Beware

Before you sit down at a Seven-Card Stud table, be aware that getting to grips with this game is going to be a real challenge. You need to learn it thoroughly before you start playing for real.

Fourth Street

The first round of betting complete, each player still in now receives another face-up card, and the second round of betting is opened by the player who has the highest one. Unless there is a pair on the board, bets in this round are, again, at increments of the lower limit.

However, if there is a pair showing (note that it doesn't have to belong to you) players have the option to bet in increments of the table's higher limit. All subsequent bets and raises will also be at this level.

Fifth Street

When the second round of betting is complete, another face-up card is dealt to the remaining players. The player with the highest card showing now starts the third betting round. Note that bets are now at the table's higher limit and will be at this level for the rest of the game.

Sixth Street

At the completion of the third round of betting, a fourth face-up card is dealt to all the players still in the game. The fourth betting round now ensues, initiated by the player with the highest face-up card.

Seventh Street

The last round is known as Seventh Street and a final card is dealt to the remaining players. This is dealt face-down. The player with the highest ranking hand on Sixth Street opens the betting and this continues until each player has folded, called or raised.

When betting is complete, players either muck their hand (concede without showing) or turn over their cards in a showdown. The highest takes the pot.

Don't forget

On Third and Fourth Street, bets are at the lower limit. From Fifth Street onwards, they are at the higher limit.

Hot tip

One of the differences between Seven-Card Stud and Texas Hold'em is that Stud has five betting rounds. This means that at comparable tables in terms of limits, the pot in Stud is usually higher.

127

Factors Specific to Seven-Card Stud

Although the hands are the same as in other forms of poker, Seven-Card Stud is unique in several respects. These are:

- There are no community cards; all players have their own

- There are five rounds of betting

- It is a more expensive game to play in terms of the forced bets (the ante and the bring-in)

- Table position changes in each betting round

- Players have to base their decisions not only on their own cards, but on those of their opponents

The fact that all the cards "belong" to the players holding them (they are not shared as in Texas Hold'em and Omaha), means that if you hit a good card that improves your hand, it won't also improve an opponent's hand. For example, in a hand of Texas Hold'em, your pocket cards are A-A and the flop and turn bring the following cards:

The ace gives you the top set but the turn card is another high card that gives anyone with a king a nut straight. In the face of a large raise, you would have to concede and fold.

This type of situation doesn't arise in Seven-Card Stud. If you get a card that improves your hand, it improves your hand only.

...cont'd

In Seven-Card Stud, there are five rounds of betting as opposed to four in Texas Hold'em. The effect of this is that more can be won on a winning hand and more lost on a losing one. While it may be easier to improve a hand in Seven-Card Stud, the attempt can be costly if it doesn't work.

The ante method of forcing players to contribute to the pot is more expensive than the blinds method used in other poker variants. In Seven-Card Stud, you have to stump up cash for each hand you play (see margin note).

In Seven-Card Stud, each betting round (apart from the first) is opened by the player who is holding the highest face-up card. This means that you never know from one round to the next where you are going to be acting from. For this reason, many players think that table position is not important. However, this is a mistake; the fact that position is not fixed in no way diminishes its importance. You just have to be flexible enough to adjust your play accordingly.

The most important factor of all is that there is a lot of information on the table, as so many cards are on display. Noting, remembering, and using this information is a crucial element in Seven-Card Stud. For example:

You are on Sixth Street (one more card to come) and you are holding four hearts – one more gives you a flush. If you have been taking note of the number of hearts in the face-up cards, you will have a very good idea of how many hearts are left in the pack (live cards). If there are not many (dead cards), the chances of making your flush are low, so you fold.

So you can see that observation, not just of the opposition but of the cards, is a much more critical factor than in Texas Hold'em or Omaha.

Hot tip

Playing ten hands at a $1.00/2.00 table will cost you $2.25 ($0.25 ante x 10). Plus, you have to pay the bring-in bet ($0.50). In total, you will pay out $2.75.

At a same limit ten-seat Texas Hold'em table where all the seats are taken, you will pay out $1.50 ($0.50 for the small blind, and $1.00 for the big blind) over ten hands.

Start Cards

The following table lists the start cards that should be played:

Top Hands
All sets: A-A-A to 2-2-2. The higher the better Pairs: A-A, K-K, Q-Q, J-J Suited connectors: A-K-Q, K-Q-J
Strong Hands
Pairs: T-T, 9-9, 8-8 Suited connectors: Q-J-T, J-T-9 Unsuited connectors: A-K-Q, K-Q-J Gapped suited connectors: A-K-J, A-Q-J
Good Hands
High three-card flush draws: e.g. Ks-7s-4s Suited connectors: T-9-8, 9-8-7, 8-7-6 Unsuited connectors: Q-J-T, J-T-9, T-9-8 Gapped suited connectors: K-Q-T, Q-J-9 Pairs: 7-7, 6-6, 5-5
Marginal Hands
Middle & low three-card flush draws: e.g. 9c-6c-2c Pairs: 4-4, 3-3, 2-2 Suited connectors: 7-6-5, 6-5-4, 5-4-3, 4-3-2 Unsuited connectors: 9-8-7, 8-7-6, 7-6-5 Gapped suited connectors: J-T-8, T-9-7 Two high cards: e.g. A-J-5, K-J-8

Hot tip

A good rule of thumb is only to play start cards that are all higher than the highest up-card on the table. This increases considerably the chances of you hitting the highest pair or two-pair.

From the table, you can see that good start cards are those that either form a complete hand (sets and high pairs) or give you both straight and flush possibilities.

However, it's not just a case of what your start cards are. Unlike Texas Hold'em, where pre-flop you have no idea what your opponents are holding, in Seven-Card Stud you can see one of their cards (the door-card) right from the off. This is an important factor when deciding whether to play a hand (and how to play it).

Playing Pairs

Third Street

On Third Street, you have your three pocket cards and can see one up-card from each player.

When considering how to play your pair, the three important factors are a) the strength of your pair, b) the up-cards and c) the strength of your kicker (the other card you were dealt).

For example, you are holding K-K-2 and your opponents' up-cards are all lower. You play this as you would in Texas Hold'em by raising to knock out opponents with drawing hands.

However, if there are players with higher up-cards than your pair, you have to be more cautious. For example, you hold 9-9-6 and an opponent showing a ten raises, only to be re-raised by one showing a queen. You can be fairly certain here that your nines are beaten, so you need another option to carry on with this hand.

The first thing to establish is whether your cards are live. If there are no 9s or 6s showing, you could call to see if you hit a set or two-pair on the next street. However, if one or more of your cards are dead, the chances of improving the hand are much diminished and you should thus fold.

You could also call if two of your cards are connected, or are of the same suit. In this case, you would have the added option of a flush or straight draw.

Many players raise automatically with any pair but if it is a low to medium pair, will usually lose as a result. The key to playing with these hands is the kicker (your third card). If it is high (A, K or Q), then the chances of success are much greater.

For example, your pocket cards are 8-8-K. You look around and see that none of these cards is showing, which means they are live. In this situation, raising is a good move.

Don't forget

In Seven-Card Stud the first thing to look for is whether the cards you need are live or dead.

...cont'd

The first thing that may happen is that no one can beat K-K and assuming from your raise that you are holding a K, the whole table folds. If your raise is called, you have a good chance of winning by hitting a set, a good two-pair, and also a high pair (K-K).

However, if your kicker is, say, a 4, the only way this hand is playable is if no one raises and all your cards are live. Otherwise, it will only get you into trouble.

Fourth Street

Each player now has two up-cards showing. You've played a high pocket pair but Fourth Street has not brought you anything. So what now?

The first thing to check is that no one has a pair in their up-cards – if they have, you could well be facing trips and be beaten already. If this is the case, you should fold to a raise assuming your pair is lower than the one on the board, your hand has no straight or flush options, or one of the other two cards of your pair is dead, e.g. you have 7-7-K and there is a 7 showing in an opponent's up-cards. Otherwise, you can call the raise and see what the next street brings.

However, if there are no paired up-cards, you can raise, especially if your cards are all live. Limping in is usually a mistake that will, in the long run, cost you money. If there is no obvious danger to your hand, you must raise to drive out players with drawing hands.

If you've played with a medium to low pair and haven't hit trips on Fourth Street, this is usually the time to fold it. However, bets are still at the lower limit at this stage of the game, so if there are no raises, and either your cards are still live or you have straight/flush possibilities, you can play on.

Fifth Street

What's the significance of Fifth Street? It's at this stage that bets double and this makes it the most important of all the streets. Mistakes from this point on are going to cost you.

As a general rule, if all you've got at this stage is just a pair, even if it's a high one, you should fold, especially in the face of heavy betting action. However, this isn't always the case and there are times when a high pair is playable.

The deciding factors here are: a) the cards you need to improve must still be live, b) you must have over-cards and c) you must have no more than two opponents.

If all of the above are in place, you can play on. If not, fold. The only exception is when the hand also offers straight or flush possibilities. Don't be tempted to stick around just because you have A-A or K-K. You will lose a lot of money with these hands if you over-play them.

Sixth Street

If you've still got no more than a pair against two or more opponents, you have to fold to a raise, particularly if another player calls the raise, or re-raises, before the action gets to you. The only exception is if you now need just one more card for a straight (a 5 to 1 shot) or flush (4 to 1 shot). It needs to be a large pot though. This is the sort of situation in which it pays to be able to work out the pot odds.

Seventh Street

By this stage, you've either improved your hand to a two-pair, trips, straight or a flush, or still just got that pair. If it's the pair, you have to fold to any raise. If there is no raise and there are no over-cards to your pair, having come this far, you should call.

Don't forget

High pairs are strong hands at the beginning but get progressively weaker as the game goes on.

Playing Sets

Third Street

Once in a blue moon, you'll have the good fortune to be dealt a three-of-a-kind in your first three cards (known as rolled-up trips).

It is very important to play this hand correctly. If you don't, it could cost you a lot of chips. Many players get dollar signs flashing in their eyes when they hit trips and will slow-play seeking to maximize the pay-off. In many cases, however, all they are achieving by doing this is actually maximizing their loss. They forget that there are several hands that can beat it – a set is by no means a guaranteed winner.

Let's say you have three 5's. With such a low set, you have to take the initiative by raising immediately. Remember, all trips, no matter how high, are vulnerable to straights and flushes. Low sets, such as our 5-5-5 example have a further disadvantage in that they are also vulnerable to higher sets. At a ten-seat table, it is not unusual to see two players both hit a set in the same hand.

So in this situation, you simply have to raise, and keep on raising, in an effort to make other players who have a higher pair in their hand fold thus denying them the chance to hit a better set than yours. If you have a high set on the other hand, Tens and above, then you can slow-play but only if there is no obvious danger of being beaten by a flush or straight. If there is, then you have to play aggressively to try and force opponents who can hit one of these hands to fold.

Fourth Street

With a high set, it is OK to keep on slow-playing if the board still looks safe (no flush or straight draws). While your set is looking as though it is the best hand, you want to build the pot by keeping in as many opponents as possible.

Also, when an opponent's up-cards are paired and the pair is lower in rank than your set, you should slow-play because there is a good chance that this player has also, or will, hit a set.

Don't forget

A set is a good hand and will take many pots. However, it only beats two hands – pairs and two-pairs. There are five hands which it doesn't beat.

Hot tip

Low sets must be played aggressively to force out opponents with straight and flush draws.

Unfortunately, for him/her, it is, or will be, a lower one than yours and you should get a big pay-off when you start raising on the later streets.

If, however, the pair is higher in rank than your set, then proceed with great caution as the boot could now be on the other foot, i.e. you are facing a higher set. The clue will be how the player bets. If there is a raise, you can call as it is at the lower limit and see what develops on Fifth Street. If the player doesn't raise, you are probably still in front (although it could well be that you are being slow-played).

In general, when in this situation on Fourth Street, call any bets but don't raise – you shouldn't be putting any more in the pot than you have to.

Should you find yourself in a situation where two opponents have a pair showing, both higher than your set, then you will have to fold to any raises. Against one player, you may well be up against nothing more than the pair on show or a two-pair, but against two opponents, you have to assume one of them has a higher set.

In situations where the board looks threatening in other ways, i.e. a possible straight or flush, your only option is to try and protect the hand by forcing the opposition to fold. The only way you can do this is by raising.

Fifth Street
It's at this stage that bets are at the higher limit. If your set still looks like it is the best hand, now is the time to start raising. Opponents hoping to hit a straight or flush will usually call and will usually miss their hand, thus presenting you with a nice pot at the end.

If, however, there is a pair showing higher in rank than your set, call any bets but don't raise. You could well be beaten here but trips is not a hand you can fold unless it's obvious you are.

Beware

Whenever there is a pair on the board higher than your set, slow down. Don't put any more in the pot than you have to because you may well be playing a dead hand.

...cont'd

For example, if one player has three suited cards showing and another has a pair higher in rank than your trips showing and both are raising, it's a fair assumption that you are beaten. In this scenario, you should fold.

Another situation in which you'd have to fold your trips is when two or more of the cards you need to improve to a full house or quads are dead. If another player is showing a three-to-a-flush or straight and is raising, it's a fairly safe assumption they have you beaten. There is no point in continuing as your chances of improving to a full house are very slim.

Sixth Street

All the players still in the hand now have 4 up-cards showing and it's becoming clearer what you are up against. An interesting point to note about Sixth Street is that by this stage, anyone still in is, to a certain extent, committed to the pot. With just one more street to go, they are generally unlikely to be shaken off their hand by a raise.

Therefore, you must be fairly certain that you currently have the best hand before raising on this street. If your trips look vulnerable but the cards you need to hit quads or a full house are still live, then just call.

Seventh Street

The last cards are now dealt face-down. Thus, you are none the wiser regarding the strength of your opponents' hands than you were at Sixth Street. The only change that you can see is to your own hand. Assuming, your trips haven't improved, your actions must be guided by what your opponents do.

If your hand still looks strong, raise – players who have missed their draw will now fold. Otherwise, call and check the hand out if possible. However, in the face of determined raising from a player with a high pair, or three or four cards to a straight or flush, you would be advised to fold. Remember, a set is a good hand but not that good.

Playing Two Pairs

Fourth Street

A two-pair hand can be a difficult one to play. It's too good to casually fold but nor is it one you can have too much confidence in. Many players will play this hand to the end knowing they are just one card away from a full house, which is not a good idea at all.

What you do depends on: a) are the cards needed to turn the two-pair into a full house, live? and, b) how high your cards are. If two or more of the cards are dead, then the hand is shaping up to be a loser. The only way you would play it is if the pairs are both high ones – tens or above, or a pair of aces with a lower pair. If both pairs are low it might be worth calling a single bet to see the next street but certainly not a raise.

If there is a pair on the board higher than both your pairs, muck the hand immediately unless you get a free card. You may well have this player beaten but with three cards still to come, there is a very good chance that he will hit another pair.

However, with a high two-pair, a raise at this stage of the game is a good move. You will certainly get some of the opposition to fold, which increases your chances of winning.

Fifth Street

Playing a two-pair is much the same as playing A-A or K-K – they are all good hands at the beginning but become progressively less so as the streets advance. The general rule is that if there are no obvious dangers (see below), protect the hand by raising to drive out players with draws.

As on Fourth Street, watch out for higher pairs on the board. As soon as you see one, this hand should be mucked. If one of the cards needed to improve to a full house falls dead and an opponent is showing two or three cards to a straight or flush, you need to exercise caution. You can't fold the hand yet but certainly don't want to be committing yourself to the pot any more than you have to.

Hot tip

Two-pairs are not a very good hand but just one card can turn them into a monster, i.e. a full house. However, the odds on this happening are not good so be wary with this hand.

...cont'd

Sixth Street

If you've been raising with your two-pair on the previous streets and still have opposition by the time you reach Sixth Street, you need to re-evaluate the situation.

If you have just one opponent and there is nothing threatening on the board then carry on raising. Your opponent is probably on a draw – if he/she misses it, which is probable, you will win a nice pot.

However, if the player raises you or re-raises your raise, then you have to consider the possibility that you are up against trips or a higher two-pair. You can't fold yet though, so just call and see what develops on Seventh Street.

If you have two or more opponents, then regardless of whether your hand looks the best, you should play more cautiously. Just check and call. You can call a single raise but faced with a re-raise, you should fold.

Seventh Street

The final card is dealt face-down so the situation here is much the same as on the previous street. You know if your hand has improved but have no indication regarding the opposition.

If an opponent raises and there is no pair showing on the board, then call the raise. However, you should probably fold to a re-raise.

In general, when on Seventh Street, unless you've been playing a drawing hand and missed your draw, you should rarely fold. If you can see the hand out without too much expense then do so.

Hot tip

When faced with two opponents who are both raising, folding a two-pair is usually the best move.

Playing Flush Draws

Third Street

One of the biggest mistakes that poker players in general make is over-playing flush draws. It's understandable as a flush is a powerful hand but the chances of hitting one are really not that good. It is a fact that if you play every suited hand you get, the losses you make in the failed attempts will exceed by a considerable margin the winnings in the few successful attempts.

Another point to make is that it is quite common to see a low ranked flush beaten by a higher one, especially at a ten-seat table.

The key to playing flush draws then is to only play them in the following circumstances:

1) When the hand contains an ace or a king so that if you hit the flush it will be a high one. The ace or king also acts as a backup by giving you a chance of a high pair

2) When the hand also has straight possibilities. So, if you miss the flush, as you probably will, there is still another way to win

Furthermore, even if condition 1 above is met, if two or more of the suit you need are dead (showing in other players' up-cards), then the chances of hitting the flush are very slim. In this situation, muck the hand immediately. However, if condition 2 is met, then it is worth playing the hand.

As regards betting, you should never raise with a flush draw. The idea is to: a) see the next card as cheaply as possible, and b) keep the opposition in the game so that if you hit the flush you are likely to get some action.

Fourth Street

If you've still got a three-to-a-flush at this stage, you want to see the next card as cheaply as you can. This means folding to a raise unless the hand has other options.

Hot tip

Only play a flush draw if the cards are high and/or offer other options should you miss the flush. If you play all the suited hands you are dealt, you are guaranteed to be a big loser.

Hot tip

You must evaluate your chances of completing a flush draw by noting how many of the cards you need are live.

...cont'd

However, if you get another of your suit giving you a four-to-a-flush, then you definitely want to stick around. The exception to this would be if there is a pair on the board, which means an opponent could have trips. Yes, if you hit the flush, you will beat the trips but those trips could well turn into a full house. In this situation, a raise from the player with the pair should have you folding.

Fifth Street

If you're still stuck with a three-to-a-flush here, this is the time to fold it. You need both of the last two cards to make your hand and it's not likely to happen. If an opponent raises then it's a no-brainer – muck the cards.

With a four-to-a-flush, you've still got a good shot at the pot, assuming no more than five of your suit are dead. If it's more, fold unless you have another hand or a good chance of making one.

Sixth Street

At this stage of the game, you have money invested in the pot and so need a good reason to fold your hand. You should have either a four-to-a-flush, or a three-to-a-flush with another good hand or draw.

If it's the former, only fold if six or more of your suit are dead, or an opponent is showing a pair and raising. If it's the latter, how you play depends on the strength, or potential strength, of the other hand and how it stacks up against the potential hands of the opposition.

Seventh Street

This should be easy. If you've hit your flush, you raise and keep raising. The only exceptions are when an opponent has a pair showing in which case you have to be wary of a full house, and when it's a low flush. In either of these situations, play the hand out as cheaply as possible. You can't fold a flush but if it's vulnerable, don't put any more on it than you have to. Of course, if you haven't hit the flush and have nothing else, simply muck the hand.

Playing Straight Draws

Third Street

Straight draws are very similar to flush draws in that you need to hit five cards to complete the hand. However, you should be aware that the chances of hitting a straight are even less than hitting a flush.

One of the most important things to remember is that the higher your straight, the better it is. Furthermore, having high cards in your hand also gives you a chance of a high pair or two-pair, thus providing another option should you miss the straight.

It goes without saying that the cards you need to complete the straight must be live. If two or more of the cards needed to improve to a four-to-a-straight are gone, fold the hand. When looking for dead cards, you should also be considering the cards that will complete the four-to-a-straight should you get that.

For example, you have Q-J-T. You need a K or a 9 to make a four-to-a-straight, so you make sure these are still live. However, if either of these do come, you will still need either an A or an 8 to complete the straight, so these cards have to be live as well.

As with flush draws, you call and check with these hands – never raise. The odds against you making the hand are high so you don't want to invest any more than you have to.

Fourth Street

If you haven't improved to a four-to-a-straight, the best option is usually to fold right here. The only exceptions are if the hand offers other options, or all the cards you need to improve are still live and you don't have to call a raise to continue.

If you do now have a four-to-a-straight, the chances of completing it by Seventh Street are about 1.5 to 1, which makes the hand playable even in the face of a raise.

Hot tip

Straight and flush draws are speculative hands and should be played as cheaply as possible. They are not hands to raise with.

141

...cont'd

Even so, if three or more of the cards you need are dead, folding isn't a bad option. Also, keep an eye open for pairs on the board. Whenever one appears, there is the possibility of an opponent already having a full house or hitting one later on.

Fifth Street

If you're still on a three-to-a-straight and have no other options, you must fold. The odds against getting both the cards you need on the final two streets are simply too great.

With a four-to-a-straight and three or more of the cards you need dead, again you have to fold unless you have another hand.

In the case of an inside straight draw, all your cards must be live. If even one is dead, muck the hand.

Sixth Street

By this stage of the game you will have committed quite a few of your chips to the pot and thus need a good reason to fold.

One is lack of live cards – you must keep count of these as the hand progresses. Another is the likelihood of an opponent making a higher straight, or a hand better than a straight. With regard to the latter, this is quite likely to happen if you play low or medium cards. Also, if someone has a pair showing and puts in a big bet.

Seventh Street

Crunch time – if you've missed the straight and have nothing else that's likely to take the pot, you fold. This is going to be the case more often than not. However, if you do have something else, e.g. a high pair, you can call a single bet but should fold to a raise.

If you've completed your hand and no one is showing a three-to-a-flush, a pair or cards that could make a higher straight than yours, you raise and keep raising. This pot you're going to win.

Beware

You should never draw to an inside straight unless there is a large pot at stake. Even with all the cards live, the chances of hitting one are very slim.

Don't forget

When going for a low to medium straight, always be aware of the possibility of hitting the low (sucker) end while an opponent has got the high end.

Playing Killer Hands

What's a killer hand? Quite simply one that cannot be beaten or is extremely unlikely to be beaten. These are full houses, four-of-a-kinds (quads) and straight flushes. Hit either of the latter two and the pot really is as good as yours.

Full houses are not quite as strong as there is often the possibility that someone has hit a higher one. However, if you only play high cards, as you should, this is rarely going to happen.

So how do you play these hands? Raise and keep raising? The answer is sometimes but more usually not. It depends on at what stage of the game you make the hand and, in the case of a full house, the strength of the cards and whether or not there is a higher pair on the board.

Let's start with quads and straight flushes. With either of these, you can consider the hand won. The only problem you face is how to get the most out of it. If you have the great good fortune to hit one on Fourth or Fifth Street and immediately start raising, most, if not all, of the opposition are simply going to fold.

This is a situation where you can, and must, slow-play with the objective of giving players with drawing hands every opportunity to make their hand. If one of them hits a flush, you are going to win a very nice pot. So just call all bets but don't raise. However, if a check comes round to you, bet – while you don't want to scare anyone off, you do want to see money going in the pot. Anyone on a draw will call a single bet – it's raises that will make them fold.

Full houses, however, are a different kettle of fish. Unless you've got aces full of kings, there is always a chance that someone will hit a higher one. This is by no means an uncommon scenario. How you play this hand depends entirely on how high your cards are.

Don't forget

It is a fact that quads and straight flushes are the only hands that you can safely slow-play. The only exception is a full house with aces full of kings.

Hot tip

When slow-playing a killer hand, never take the check option. You must get your opponents' money into the pot.

...cont'd

For example, you've got nines full of eights (9-9-9-8-8) on Fifth Street. This is a great hand.

An opponent is showing J-6 and bets. You decide to slow-play and just call. Sixth Street brings this player a 6 and, again, you call. Seventh Street brings another J and now you are looking at J-J-6. Now, at last, you raise and are immediately re-raised. Assuming you are facing trips, you raise straight back and are re-raised again, which is just what you want.

At the showdown, however, your opponent reveals pocket cards of 2-J-6. Your full house has been beaten by a higher one.

The lesson here is that with a full house comprised of low or medium cards, you can never assume that the pot is as good as won, as you would with quads and straight flushes. Unless, it is made up of aces, kings or queens, it is a big mistake to slow-play a full house. You have to raise and keep on raising to force opponents holding higher cards to fold and deny them the chance to get lucky, which, every now and again, they will.

However, if your full house is made up of kings full of queens, you can be ninety nine per cent certain of winning the hand, and thus could slow-play it.

Should you ever fold one of these hands? The answer is yes but very, very rarely. Lets say you're on Seventh Street and holding 7-7-7-8-8. You have two opponents both showing higher pairs. One raises and the other re-raises. You call the raise and the first player raises again. The second player re-raises the first. Now it's you to play.

Alarm bells must be going off in your head. You couldn't be too sure of this hand against one raiser, never mind two. In this situation, folding is not a bad option to take.

10 Tournaments

To win poker tournaments, you need to play with a different strategy from that you'd use in cash games. This chapter shows you how.

146 Introduction

147 Types of Tournament

151 Prize Money

152 Chip Stacks

154 Multi-Table Strategy

157 Single-Table Strategy

159 Heads-Up Strategy

Introduction

Tournaments are rapidly becoming one of the most popular forms of poker – many people play nothing else. One of the reasons for this is the extensive television coverage they receive. Another is the fact that you "know where you are" with them. You know exactly how much it's going to cost to enter and you have a good idea of how long it will take.

So what exactly is a poker tournament? Basically, it's a game of elimination. Each entrant buys in for a fixed amount and the total buy-in forms the prize pool. In addition, the poker room charges each entrant a fee that, typically, is 10% of the buy-in (this is how the poker room makes its money).

As the tournament progresses, players lose their chips and are eliminated until just one remains. Typically, this player will win 20-30% of the pool.

There are many different types of tournament and the main ones include:

- Heads-up
- Multi-table (MTT)
- Single-table (STT)
- Sit-and-go
- Rebuy
- Satellite
- Freeroll
- Private

All poker rooms have most, if not all, of the tournament types listed above on offer. Some, like the multi-table affairs, have a fixed starting time and are pre-announced. The sit-and-go type, on the other hand, are ready as soon as the last player has taken a seat.

Tournaments are available for all the variations of poker. The most popular is Texas Hold'em (both fixed- and no-limit) but you will also find them for Five- and Seven-Card Stud, and Omaha.

Beware

Televised poker tournaments need to be taken with a pinch of salt. What many people fail to realize is that they are seeing only the best of the action. The rest is edited out.

Hot tip

There are quite a few websites that offer updated lists of upcoming tournaments from the major online poker rooms. An example is www.texasholdem-poker.com. Click "Online Poker Tournies" on the menu at the left.

Types of Tournament

Multi-Table (MTT)

If you want to win serious money playing poker, multi-table tournaments are the way to do it. However, there will be several hundreds, or even thousands, of other players all with the same thing in mind. You will need skill and a very large slice of luck to come out on top. Indeed, luck is without doubt the single most important factor in any given tournament. Yes, you need to be a good player (which is why the same players consistently reach the final stages of the World Series of Poker), but to actually win also requires that good fortune is on your side on that particular day.

The first step is to register for the tournament, at which time you pay the tournament's buy-in fee. When the registration period is over, each entrant is allocated a seat at a table. Using a 200-player tournament as an example, there will be 20 tables, each seating ten players. When the tournament is due to begin, a window will open up on your screen (online tournaments) with the table at which you've been seated. In live poker rooms there will be an electronic board that displays this information.

Each player is allocated the same number of chips, usually 1500. At the beginning of the tournament (level one), the blinds are at a very low level, typically $10/20. However, at specific intervals (these vary, but we'll use a typical figure of 15 minutes as an example), they increase. When this happens the tournament is said to have moved to level two. 15 minutes later, the blinds increase again and the tournament is at level three. After four hours, the tournament will be at level 16, and the blinds will be in the region of $4000/8000.

As players lose their chips and are eliminated, remaining players are moved to different tables and redundant tables are closed. This is known as rebalancing. When only ten players remain, they are all seated at the final table.

Play continues until all but one has been eliminated.

...cont'd

Don't forget

Satellite tournaments offer a cheap route into the big money tournaments. Most of the major online poker rooms run satellite tournaments that lead to the WSOP.

Hot tip

Many players will do an immediate rebuy. This doubles their stack and gives them an advantage over the players who don't. However, they will have invested twice as much.

Satellites

A satellite is basically a small tournament within a large tournament. There is no cash prize; instead, the winner gets a free seat at the next stage (known as a super-satellite) of the main tournament. The goal is to win through to the final table of the tournament. The advantage of the satellite is that, for a very small initial entry fee, it is possible to end up at a table where the buy-in can be several thousand dollars. The most well-known example of this is the World Series of Poker Championship. To buy a seat in the final stages of this tournament costs some $10,000. If you can get there via satellites, though, it will cost you a fraction of that amount.

Rebuys and Add-Ons

Rebuy tournaments are those in which players can buy more chips if they wish to. So if you lose your initial stack, rather than busting out of the tournament, you can buy another stack.

However, rebuys are restricted to specific periods (known as rebuy periods, surprisingly). Typically, these last an hour and usually occur in the early stages of the tournament. In some cases, the rebuy period is not time-limited but will be specified in terms of levels of the tournament. For example, rebuys may be allowed in levels one, two and three.

You don't need to have lost your initial stack before you can rebuy. Some poker rooms allow you to rebuy if your stack is equal to or less than the initial stack. This means that you can do an immediate rebuy before the first card is dealt (see margin note). Sometimes, a rebuy is permitted only when a player's stack has dropped to half, or less, of its initial size. The conditions vary according to the poker room and the tournament.

Add-ons are one-off opportunities to purchase more chips, and are offered at intervals throughout the tournament. There are no restrictions as there are with rebuys. Regardless of your stack size, you can buy more.

Single-Table (STT)

These tournaments are probably the most popular of all. Usually, they are restricted to ten or six players, and as soon as the last player has taken a seat, the tournament begins.

The beauty of single-table tournaments (and one reason that they're so popular) is that they are quick – most are completed within an hour. This means that you don't have to take the entire afternoon off as you would with a multi-table tournament.

The other big advantage is that you only have a few opponents to beat to finish in the money. Therefore, your chances of at least recouping the buy-in are good. The prize money, typically, is as follows:

- First place takes 50% of the prize pool
- Second place takes 30%
- Third place takes 20%

There are also plenty of these tournaments running. As soon as you've finished one, you can sit down at another.

Heads-Up

In a heads-up tournament, players are pitched against single opponents. Winners advance to the next stage of the tournament where they face another single opponent. At no time are there more than two players at a table.

Private

Most poker rooms allow you to set up a private tournament in which only players specified by you can take part.

It can be any type of game (Hold'em, Omaha, Seven-Card Stud, etc.), and you can specify the tournament's parameters yourself. These include the buy-in, the blinds levels, the prize distribution, and the number of starting chips.

Hot tip

The big advantage of STTs is that they are very quick. You also have a much greater chance of finishing in the prize money.

Beware

Heads-up poker is very difficult to master. See page 159 for more details on this.

...cont'd

Freeroll

Offered only by online poker rooms, a freeroll is a tournament where there is no cash buy-in, but the winners receive cash or some other kind of worthwhile prize (for example, free entry to a cash tournament).

While the poker rooms lose money on these events, they offer them for two reasons: a) as a means of enticing people into their sites, and b) to reward loyal players (it's an incentive to keep their custom).

To play in any freeroll tournament, a player must have an account at the site in question and also, in most cases, must have made a previous cash deposit and played a certain number of raked hands. The poker rooms are not in the business of giving money away, so, not surprisingly, prizes tend to be less than spectacular. Typical figures range from $20 to $500. The higher the money on offer, the more entrants there will be. It's quite common to see several thousand players battling it out for the higher amounts.

Are they worth it? Well, this depends on why you play poker. Certainly, they can be an enjoyable way of passing an hour or two, with the added bonus of a possible prize at the end. If you are thinking of them as a way of making money, though, think again. Typically, winners get about 25% of the prize pool, so in a $200 tournament, the first prize will be in the region of $50. This is not much to show for what may take several hours of your time (assuming you win).

From a practical viewpoint, their only real worth is as an introduction to real money tournament play. As with all free-money tables though, you have to take what you see with a pinch of salt. Players do the craziest things in freerolls. If you play them often enough, some of this craziness might start rubbing off on you and become part of your real money game.

In essence, then, freerolls are fun and, for newcomers to tournament play, can be instructive to a certain degree.

Prize Money

When a tournament is over, the prize money is distributed. The table below shows how prize pools are split for tournaments of all sizes. The figures are percentages (and are approximate):

Players	1 to 30	31 to 50	51 to 100	101 to 200	201 to 400	401 to 600	601 to 800	801 to 1000	1001 plus
1st	50.00	40.00	30.00	27.50	25.00	25.00	25.00	25.00	22.50
2nd	30.00	24.00	20.00	17.00	16.00	15.00	14.50	14.00	12.50
3rd	20.00	16.00	12.00	11.50	10.50	9.50	9.25	9.00	8.50
4th		12.00	9.25	8.50	8.00	7.00	6.75	6.50	6.50
5th		8.00	7.50	7.25	7.00	6.00	5.75	5.50	5.25
6th			6.25	5.75	5.50	5.00	4.75	4.50	4.25
7th			5.25	4.50	4.50	4.00	3.75	3.50	3.25
8th			4.25	3.00	3.00	3.00	2.75	2.50	2.25
9th			3.25	2.00	1.75	1.75	1.75	1.50	1.50
10th			2.25	2.00	1.25	1.25	1.25	1.00	1.00
11-15				1.20	0.95	0.95	0.95	0.90	0.85
16-20				1.10	0.75	0.75	0.75	0.70	0.65
21-30					0.50	0.50	0.50	0.50	0.45
31-40					0.40	0.35	0.35	0.35	0.35
41-50						0.30	0.30	0.30	0.30
51-60						0.25	0.25	0.25	0.25
61-70							0.20	0.20	0.20
71-90							0.15	0.15	0.15
91-110								0.10	0.10
111-150									0.10

Hot tip

Some tournaments incorporate a bounty feature. This adds another element to a standard tournament by having some players carry a bounty on their heads. If you eliminate any of them from the tournament you will receive a bounty bonus.

From the table we can see that the more entrants there are in a tournament, the more ways the prize pool is split. We can also see that to be in the prize money it is usually necessary to finish in the final 10% approximately.

However, to win a worthwhile amount of money it is usually necessary to finish in the final 3 or 4%.

Chip Stacks

The number of chips you have is very important. This may seem an obvious statement, but we are talking about knock-out tournaments here. Run out of chips in a cash game and there is nothing to stop you buying some more. In a tournament, however, with no chips you're out of the game (unless it's a rebuy).

The size of your stack also has a big influence on the way you play, and there are several reasons for this:

First, in a multi-table tournament where you are facing hundreds or even thousands of opponents, it is essential to know where you stand in relation to the opposition. You may have the most chips at your table, but what about all the other tables? Are you in 8th place overall, or is it 800th? If it's 8th then you are doing well and may decide to consolidate your position by playing conservatively for a while. If it's 800th though, you may well need to do the opposite in an attempt to improve your position.

Second, in a tournament a large stack buys you power. It allows you to play more aggressively and intimidate opponents who are short-stacked.

Third, if you are short-stacked you face another, more relentless, opponent: the blinds. Unless you increase your stack, and soon, they will swallow you up. You will be much more susceptible to the vagaries of luck, and vulnerable to the power-plays of opponents with larger stacks. In this situation, your strategy has to change. Faced with imminent elimination, caution is no longer an option; you will have to change tack and adopt a high-risk strategy.

So how do you know your position in relation to the others? In a live tournament, you don't until you reach the latter stages and can then see how many are left. Online poker software, however, gives you this information in the game window or in the tournament lobby.

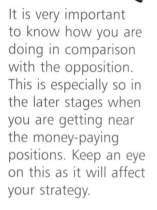

Hot tip

It is very important to know how you are doing in comparison with the opposition. This is especially so in the later stages when you are getting near the money-paying positions. Keep an eye on this as it will affect your strategy.

152

...cont'd

An example from Poker Stars is shown below:

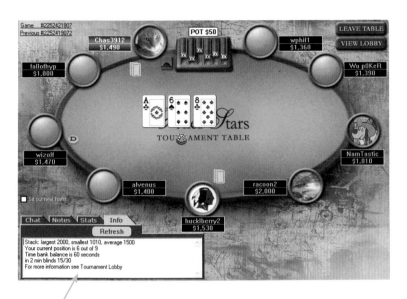

Hot tip

Being able to see instantly how you are doing in a tournament is extremely useful. Poker software that doesn't provide this information in the game window should be avoided, particularly if you intend to play a lot of tournaments.

Here, you can see your current position in the tournament, the number of players remaining, and details of the other players' stacks – highest, lowest and average, and the level of the blinds

More detailed information on the tournament will be found in the tournament lobby

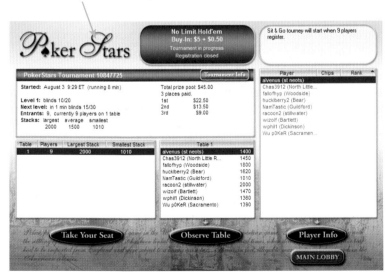

Multi-table Strategy

The strategy described below is the best way to play these tournaments.

Early Stages

The general rule is to play a very tight game to begin with. You don't want to be making any risky plays until you have evaluated the opposition.

In the early stages of any tournament there will be a good number of bad, impatient, and aggressive players hoping to gain an early advantage. To this end, they will be going all-in with high pairs and Ax hands. These are precisely the sort of players you want to avoid early on; let them eliminate themselves.

Play nothing but A-A, K-K, Q-Q, J-J and A-K suited; fold everything else. If you don't get any of these hands, don't worry about it. It doesn't matter too much if you don't play a single hand at this stage. Remember, all you'll be losing is a small amount in the blinds. While you are doing this, many of your opponents will be doing the opposite and getting themselves busted out, or short-stacked.

Even hands like A-Q and K-Q are not worth playing. In cash games, you would bet hard on these hoping to knock out the opposition. In the early stages of a tournament, however, several players are likely to call your bet. As a result, you may well end up trapping yourself with the second-best hand.

Having said all this, don't pass up the opportunity provided if you get A-A. With these cards you should definitely go all-in. Although it may not work, resulting in an early bust-out, remember that you are always the favorite to win in this situation. More often than not, you will win the hand and double-up. When you do, you will be in a strong position. This is how tournaments are won.

Bluffing is also something you should avoid. At this stage there will be too many players who are likely to call one.

Hot tip

Playing a very tight game initially has benefits at the later stages. Your opponents will put you down as a rock, and will continue to do so for a good while after you open up with your big guns.

Beware

Do not try any bluffing maneuvers early on. There will still be many bad players in the game to whom a bluff means nothing. They will simply call your bet, thus placing you in a difficult situation.

Middle Stage

At this point, most of the maniacs and otherwise bad players will have been eliminated. The few that are left will be the ones who got lucky. The remainder will be mostly reasonable players with a sprinkling of good ones.

Now is the time to loosen up and play a still tight, but more aggressive, game. You need to start winning some pots now for two reasons: a) to keep the blinds (which are now becoming more of a threat) at bay and, b) to have a decent stack for when you reach the final table. Whereas before you were playing only the top hands, now you should be playing a greater range of hands, and playing them aggressively.

Your tight play early on will have convinced the opposition that you don't take risks. Also, they will now be better players who are more likely to respect a bluff. So you are now perfectly placed to try this tactic. Short-stacked players are the obvious target here. The longer the tournament goes on, the more of a threat the blinds become to them. Use your large stack to pressurize them into making mistakes. This is the ideal situation in which to use the all-in bet. If you lose, you lose some; if they lose, they lose it all.

With the blinds at a decent level, this provides another opportunity to increase your stack by stealing them. This is where your tight table image will again be useful.

As you approach the latter stages, you need to evaluate your position. Use the software (if playing online) to see how you stand in relation to players at the other tables. If you're well below the average then you need to start taking some risks to improve your position. If your stack is at a critical level in relation to the blinds, go all-in on the first half-decent hand you get – any pair or Ax will do.

As the final table approaches, keep a close eye on the opposition. For example, if there are 15 players left and 5 of them have much lower stacks than you then play safe; they are the ones unlikely to make it.

Hot tip

To win a tournament, you will need to take calculated gambles. If you don't do this, while you may well hang in to the later stages, you will rarely reach a money-paying position.

Hot tip

With the blinds at a much higher level, try and steal them when you are in late position. This can be a useful way of maintaining your stack. Don't try this in the early stages of the tournament, though. You are more likely to be called by bad players, plus the size of the blinds won't be high enough to make it worthwhile.

...cont'd

Final Table

Depending on the size of the tournament, you will usually be in the money already. However, finishing tenth is not usually going to win you much – every position you gain now is going to increase your winnings considerably. How you approach this final stage of the game is largely dependent on how many chips you have.

High/Medium Stack

Take no risks initially; in particular, avoid confrontations with other large-stacked players. These players tend to play either aggressively to kill off the opposition, or tightly in an attempt to outlast them. Don't get involved with the former unless you have a very good hand. The latter, however, are susceptible to bluffs and blind stealing. Basically, just sit tight for a while and let the opposition thin itself out.

When there are four or five players left, start playing more aggressively. You need to start winning some pots now to stay ahead of the blinds and retain "stack power". You should be looking to attack short-stacked players with large bets whenever possible. They are your target and you should always try to eliminate them before they get a chance to get back in the game.

Short-Stack

The advice here is to make a move while you still have enough chips to make it effective. The biggest mistake you can make in this situation is to leave it too late to try and get back in the game. If you do it early enough then one or two calculated gambles or bluffs could do the trick. If you leave it too late, though, the all-in bet becomes the only option. Even if you win, the amount you win will not usually be enough as you have only a few chips left.

When there's just one opponent left, you're in a heads-up situation. Here, an experienced player will beat an inexperienced one every time. If you intend to play a lot of tournaments, heads-up play is something you need to master.

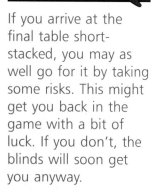

Hot tip

If you arrive at the final table short-stacked, you may as well go for it by taking some risks. This might get you back in the game with a bit of luck. If you don't, the blinds will soon get you anyway.

Single-Table Strategy

Early Stages

A single-table tournament rarely lasts more than hour. For this reason, unlike in a multi-table tournament, you cannot just sit and wait for top hands because they might never come.

The first point to make is that the blinds are at their lowest at the beginning of the tournament, which means you can see speculative hands, such as suited connectors and low pairs that you would normally fold, without making much of a dent in your stack. If you manage to hit your hand, you will often bust an opponent with a high pair and double-up very early in the game. This sets you up nicely, as you can then sit back for a while and watch the others bust themselves.

With big hands like A-A, K-K, Q-Q, A-K, A-Q and K-Q, it's important to play them correctly. With these hands you should raise five to six times the big blind. What you are hoping to get here is one caller who either hits the same pair as you but with a lower kicker, or a lower pair, and is prepared to commit himself to the pot with it. What you must not do is make a feeble raise that encourages players with drawing hands to call.

If you don't hit the flop with hands such as A-K, A-Q and K-Q, just let them go as you haven't invested too much in the pot. However, if you do hit top pair with any of the aforementioned hands, you will usually have the best hand and should be prepared to back it up with your entire stack, should it come to that.

Middle Stages

As the blinds go up, your starting hand selection should become more conservative. With every player that busts out, drawing hands progressively lose their value because usually there are not enough players in the pot to warrant playing them. Also, the stakes are now too high to be playing speculative hands such as these.

Hot tip

The blinds in a ten-seat single-table tournament, typically, are as shown below:

Level 1 – $15/30
Level 2 – $30/60
Level 3 – $50/100
Level 4 – $100/200
Level 5 – $200/400
Level 6 – $400/600
Level 7 – $600/1200
Level 8 – $1000/2000

...cont'd

Assuming your stack is in good shape, restrict yourself to playing the top hands and medium to high pairs. While you are doing this, more opponents will be busting out.

However if your stack is not looking too good, you will need to take any reasonable opportunity to rebuild it. To this end, going all-in with any pocket pair, ten or above, or A-K and A-Q is not a bad move. These are strong hands and will usually be a favorite if you get a caller. Plus, of course, your opponents will often fold and you build your stack without having to show the hand.

Late Stages

If your stack is higher than the average, you can afford to play a waiting game – with a bit of luck you may get into the money by just sitting tight. If you do play a hand, unless it's a monster, avoid confrontations with opponents who have higher stacks – you do not want to bust out while there are players with smaller stacks.

However, if you are short-stacked, there is no point in sitting there passively while the blinds gobble up your few remaining chips. Going all-in with any pair or Ax hand will very often get you out of trouble.

Once you're down to two opponents, aggression is the key. With the blinds at a high level, taking uncontested pots by going all-in at every opportunity will rapidly build your stack.

Many players at this stage will be looking to finish at least second and will often back down in the face of raw aggression. Any hand with an ace or a king, or a pocket pair should see all your chips in the middle.

When you are down to just one opponent, you are in a heads-up situation – the next page tells you how to bust him out as well.

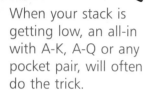

Hot tip

When your stack is getting low, an all-in with A-K, A-Q or any pocket pair, will often do the trick.

Heads-Up Strategy

With ten opponents, you can play a tight game and still stay ahead of the blinds. With five opponents, they come around twice as fast and waiting for top hands is no longer an option – you have to make a move with lesser hands.

With just one opponent, the blinds are hitting your stack every single hand. This means you have no choice – you have to play nearly every one. As the blinds are now at a very high level, three or four successive folds will see your opponent's stack rocketing upwards and yours plummeting. This is something that you cannot allow to happen, so you have to steal pots with nothing hands.

The key to this situation is to keep your opponent permanently under pressure. In heads-up play, the first player to make a move will usually take the pot, so this has to be you. Accordingly, you should raise at least 75% of the time when you're first to act. It doesn't matter what cards you have because your opponent is going to fold more often than not.

If your bluff is called, just fold. You should also raise frequently when you are last to act. Remember, with just two players, the odds are that in any one hand both of you are sitting there with nothing. The most aggressive player will usually be the one who takes the pot.

Of course, when you raise with nothing, you shouldn't over-cook it. There will be times when you are called or re-raised and you're going to have to back down. Just raise enough to make your opponent think hard about calling with a marginal hand.

The other big advantage of this style of play is that when you do get a very good hand, you can trap your opponent with the check-raise. When you suddenly check after a series of raises, the assumption will be that you have a weak hand at best and this will usually trigger an attempt to steal. Then you can raise and take a nice pot.

159

Hot tip

When deciding whether to play or fold a starting hand against one opponent, a J-7 hand is a good reference. Every hand higher than this, statistically, will be the favorite to win.

Hot tip

To win at heads-up poker, you simply must play aggressively; it gives you a big advantage. If you allow your opponent to gain the initiative, you will be on the back foot.

...cont'd

Now it may be that you are up against an equally aggressive player. Does this mean you should adopt a less aggressive stance? Absolutely not. In heads-up situations, the most aggressive player will triumph far more often than not. So do the opposite – re-raise your opponent's raises. Very often, he will back down.

Having said all this, if you are faced with a maniac who is aggressive to the point of stupidity (and there are many of these about), the opposite tack will usually pay dividends. Maniacs will often go all-in rather than put in a measured raise and by calling, you are putting yourself at risk of being busted. Basically, it becomes a crap-shoot where the outcome is decided purely by luck.

The trick here is to simply wait until you have any pair, or an ace or a king. Then call the all-in if it comes. Sometimes, you will still lose, even if you have the better hand, but usually you won't. You still have to play aggressively yourself, of course, but with a greater degree of caution than you might otherwise employ. An opponent who over-does the all-ins is a ripe peach waiting to be plucked.

The two most important factors in heads-up poker are your style of play and getting a read on your opponent. If he/she is a passive player, raw aggression will take them down. If they are the opposite, then a more measured approach should be taken. It is also nice to get some good cards but even with hand after hand of rubbish, it is still possible to come out on top.

One other point is that the further ahead you are, the more aggressively you should play. The more short-stacked your opponent becomes, the less inclined he or she will be to bet and thus you'll win many uncontested pots.

If you are the short-stacked one, the all-in bet is your way back into the game.

11 Improving Your Game

This chapter shows you ways you can improve the way you play. This is something you should always be striving to do.

162 Practice, Practice, Practice

163 Poker Simulation Software

164 Keep Records

165 Analyze Your Game

165 Poker Analysis Software

166 How to Avoid Going On Tilt

Practice, Practice, Practice

The only way to become really proficient at something is to work at it – everybody knows this but few have the willpower and self-discipline to actually do it.

Poker is no different. The great players didn't become great overnight. Years of hard work (studying and analyzing the game), constant travelling, late nights, etc., lie behind their success.

Assuming you aren't aiming to be a pro, you have it much easier. The main thing you need to become a winning poker player – experience – is literally at your fingertips. All you have to do is log on to a online poker room and play for as long as is necessary to understand the strategies explained in books such as this one, and develop the discipline to apply them. Furthermore, by sticking to the micro-limit tables, if, initially, you lose, the losses will be negligible.

All online poker rooms provide play-money tables and many poker books suggest that these are the ideal place to learn the game without any financial risk. We disagree, for two reasons:

1) Poker *is* a game of financial risk, and if your mistakes aren't costing you hard cash, you are likely to keep on making them

2) Because there is no real money involved, players at these tables make the most ridiculous moves – ones that would quickly bankrupt them if they tried them at a real money table. An essential part of poker is learning how to read your opponents and how to handle the various styles of play (tight, aggressive, passive, etc.). At play-money tables, all you will encounter is the maniac. In short, you will learn very little that's useful. The only thing we can find in their favor is that they do allow you to get the hang of the software and develop a feel for the mechanics of the online game

Once you've done this, though, move on to the low- or micro-limit tables and get your practice in there.

Poker Simulation Software

You will find that there are many computer programs that let you practice your game on the PC. Probably the best one is from Wilson Software. This company provides a program for each of the main poker games found in poker rooms – Texas Hold'em, Omaha, and Seven-Card Stud. There is also a version for Texas Hold'em tournament play. We'll take a brief look at their "Turbo Texas Hold'em" program.

The set-up screen is shown below:

The main thing with this program is that it can be configured to accurately create any table condition that you will find in the real world. For example: the number of players, the "tightness" or "looseness" of play, and parameters such as the rake, the blinds, and table limits.

If you find yourself struggling against loose players, you can construct a table full of them. If you want to learn how to play against tight players, or a combination of loose and tight, as found in many low-limit tables, this can be set up as well. Want to practice playing heads-up? Just select one opponent.

This program is highly recommended.

Keep Records

Government departments are addicted to records and statistics – they love them. These endless lists of data tell them all sorts of useful things – trends, patterns, opinions, etc. Businesses use them as well to see who's buying what, where they're buying, when they're buying, and so on. It enables them to spot problem areas, new opportunities, and get a handle on how to improve sales, etc.

As a serious poker player, you are also in business, and if government and multi-national companies feel the need to keep records, so should you. These should include:

- The date and start/end time of each session
- The amount you win or lose
- The poker rooms in which you play
- The games you play
- The table limits
- Notes on good and bad players you encounter
- Mistakes you make

The most important thing that this will do is to force you to confront reality in the event that you are losing consistently. It will be there in black and white – the amount of money you've lost (many players quickly lose track of their losses and would be horrified if they knew exactly how much).

By referring to your records, you will be able to see exactly when the money is being lost, where it is being lost, and to whom it is being lost. For example, you may notice that you are losing large amounts at a specific poker room, which perhaps indicates that the players here are hard to beat. You may do better at a different one. Or it might be that you are winning at lower-limit tables and losing at higher ones. Your results may be better at Omaha than they are at Texas Hold'em. You may win more in short sessions than in long ones. By keeping a detailed record of your poker sessions, all this information will be available, and you will find it to be extremely useful.

Analyze Your Game

The only way to pinpoint the leaks in your game is to analyze your strategy, and to do this you need statistical data on your poker sessions. Live poker rooms do not provide this information; however, online poker rooms do. This is in the form of hand histories, which can be downloaded to the PC.

Poker Analysis Software

The problem is making sense of it all. Over a typical three-hour online session, you will have played between 150 and 200 hands of poker. That's an awful lot of data to wade through. Once again, computer software comes to the rescue. Hand analysis programs take the hand history data, assimilate it, and in a matter of seconds, present you with all the relevant statistics.

There are quite a few hand analysis programs but the most well-known one is Poker Tracker. The information provided by this program is awesome and is, quite simply, everything you could possibly need.

The following is just some of the data Poker Tracker will provide:

- How many times you raise, call, check and fold. Also, where you make these actions (pre-flop, flop, river, etc.)

- How much you win and lose in each table position

- How many times you hit each type of hand (flush, straight, etc.,) and how much you win and lose with them

- Every player you have played against, plus details of their actions. It also tells you which players you have won the most from and the ones who have won the most from you

- A detailed analysis of each session, or tournament, that you play

Hot tip

Poker Tracker will replay any hand for you, as shown left. This works in the same way as a movie player, i.e. it provides playback controls, such as play and pause. This allows you to see exactly where you went wrong in the hand, so that next time, you won't make the mistake again.

You can also replay entire sessions and tournaments.

Hot tip

We saw on page 164 how keeping a record of your sessions can help you to identify general problem areas. Poker analysis software takes this to another level by pin-pointing specific weaknesses in the way you play the hands.

How to Avoid Going On Tilt

A player who is on tilt is, quite simply, one who has lost the plot, and instead of playing good solid poker, plays trash hands, bets when folding is the sensible option and vice versa. The problem is compounded if the other players notice this, as they will take ruthless advantage. This is the worst thing that can happen to a poker player. Those who keep on playing in this state will lose big-time. All the good work put in over a period of hours can be undone in minutes.

It is absolutely essential that you are aware of this issue and know how to avoid it. This means understanding *why* it happens, and the rather simplistic answer is that it's always down to negative emotions. It could be anger, frustration, impatience or even just simple boredom; it really doesn't matter which. The key, therefore, is to try to avoid any situation that is likely to trigger a negative emotional response. The two most common ones are:

The Bad-Beat
Unfortunately, this is something that cannot be avoided – it happens to all players. Forget it and move on. Play the next few hands conservatively until the memory has faded. Do not try and win it back immediately as so many do.

Lack of Progress
You've been playing for hours and your stack keeps going up and down. You never get far enough ahead to be able to say to yourself "That's a nice profit for the day, I'll stop now". Eventually, you become frustrated and start playing loosely. As you start to lose as a result, you play worse. This is an insidious form of on tilt, as it is so gradual you're not aware that it's happening. The result, nevertheless, is just as deadly.

The answer is to call a halt to the proceedings before the process begins. This is where you have to know yourself; only you know your emotional thresholds. If you're the type who gets frustrated quickly, set yourself an appropriate session period, say two hours. If you're not getting anywhere, stop playing after the two hours is up and take a break. Then have another go a bit later on.

 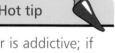

12 Miscellaneous Poker Topics

Here we cover a range of poker-related topics. You will also find a useful list of recommended reading material.

168 Other Poker Games

169 How Much Can You Win?

170 Handling Winning & Losing Streaks

172 The World Series of Poker (WSOP)

174 Cheating

176 Poker Resources

Other Poker Games

Crazy Pineapple

Crazy Pineapple is yet another variation of Texas Hold'em. While the rules and the betting structure are basically the same, there are two important differences:

1) Players are dealt *three* start cards

2) Following the second round of betting after the three flop cards are dealt, each player has to discard one of their start cards

This can result in some interesting situations. For example, say your start cards are 8-8-J and the flop brings 10-9-8. You have a set and, also, a nice outside straight draw. But, because you have to discard one of your three start cards, you have to choose which hand to play. In all other respects, the game is the same as Texas Hold'em.

Lowball

Lowball is basically Five-Card Draw poker with the difference that players are aiming to make the lowest hand – 1-2-3-4-5. It is also common for a joker to be included in the pack and this can be used as a wild card.

Players are dealt five cards face-down after which a round of betting takes place. All bets at this stage are at the lower limit. Players can then discard (burn) as many of their cards as they like and replace them with new ones. The second round of betting now ensues at the higher limit. Any players left in at the end of this reveal their cards in the showdown.

Razz

Razz is basically Seven-Card Stud, the main difference being that the lowest hand wins the pot.

In Razz, flushes and straights have no value, so the best possible hand is 5-4-3-2-A (the wheel) and is the best hand that you can make. Note that Razz is not like Hi/Lo games where split pots come into effect, e.g. Omaha Hi/Lo. It is not necessary for all cards to be under 8.

Hot tip

If you want to play any of the games mentioned on this page online, Poker Stars is the place to go.

How Much Can You Win?

A well known saying in poker is that it's a hard way to win easy money. What this basically means is that while it's not difficult to win money once you've acquired the necessary skills, it's not so easy to win worthwhile amounts.

The first thing you should do is forget everything you've seen on television regarding poker. Here, you will see players winning and losing thousands of dollars on a single hand. While it's real enough, it's very far from being typical. Many thousands of people have been attracted to poker after watching the televised poker events, no doubt thinking that there's no reason they can't do the same themselves.

If you're thinking along the same lines, or have visions of giving up the day-job, consider this: a typical poker professional playing fixed-limit Texas Hold'em in a live poker room expects to win approximately one big bet an hour (a big bet is defined as the bigger of the two table limits). For example, at a $10.00/20.00 table, it will be $20. To be clear: the player doesn't expect to win this sum *every* hour, but to *average* it. There'll be ups and downs, but overall, it will be a consistent win rate.

With online poker, it's somewhat different. First, the average online player (who's not a professional) can expect to have a lower win rate. However, this is counterbalanced by two factors: a) at least twice as many hands are dealt in an online game in any given period, and b) the standard of the opposition is generally much lower. So assuming you are good enough, at the low-limit tables you should be able to win an average of three or four big bets an hour. The higher up the limits you go, though, the lower this figure will be.

The important thing to take from this is that you should keep your expectations at a realistic level. Poker is not going to make you rich overnight. Most players simply have no idea of what constitutes a successful poker session and will often ruin a good one by playing on long after they should have stopped.

Hot tip

As a very rough guide, playing a $1.00/2.00 table for eight hours over several days should result in average winnings in the region of $50-60 per day. Don't expect to achieve this every day, though. Some days you'll lose $50, and other days you'll win $100.

Handling Winning & Losing Streaks

Everyone who plays poker will experience periods when they can do no wrong and periods when absolutely nothing goes right. This happens to the best and worst of players – no one is immune.

Winning Streaks

"What's there to think about here?" you may ask. "If I'm winning, where's the problem?" The answer is that while there is no immediate problem, there are two important considerations:

The first concerns *why* you are winning. If it is due to sheer luck rather than skilful play, then your winning streak is unlikely to last long. When it ends, all of a sudden those wonderful hands that were coming one after the other, and winning you pot after pot, will quickly become a distant memory. Now you won't be able to hit a pair, never mind a flush. What few good hands you do get will invariably be beaten by a better hand.

The point we are making here is that confusing good fortune for good play is a big mistake. By all means ride your luck, but be aware that if you can only win when the cards are falling for you, you are destined to be a loser in the long term.

The second potential problem is that of over-confidence. When everything is going right for you, it is very easy to fall into the trap of thinking everything will continue going right. Take advantage of good fortune certainly but don't let it blind you to reality, and never let yourself become so confident that you start playing carelessly.

Losing Streaks

How you handle the inevitable losing streak is probably as important as having a high level of skill. It's easy to win when the cards are falling for you, but it's not so easy to keep the money when they are against you.

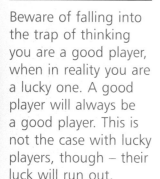

Beware

Beware of falling into the trap of thinking you are a good player, when in reality you are a lucky one. A good player will always be a good player. This is not the case with lucky players, though – their luck will run out.

170

The only thing you can do in this situation is minimize your losses as far as possible by just sitting tight until things improve. Simply fold every single hand until the cards start falling for you again. Alternatively, drop down to a micro-limit table where you can lose only a few dollars, and play out the losing streak there.

Unfortunately, most players do the opposite. Instead of playing fewer hands, or none at all, they play even more in an attempt to get their losses back quickly. This has a compound effect that results in them losing even more, and at a faster rate. As their losses mount, they become increasingly desperate and start taking absurd risks.

The other thing that often happens is players deciding to play at a higher-limit table, reasoning that with a bit of luck, they'll get their money back quickly. Even worse, they'll take their chances at a no-limit table. Unfortunately, nothing will change – playing a high- or no-limit table will not improve their luck. They'll just go bankrupt even more quickly. This is something that you must not do.

You also need to be aware that the other players will see what is happening. If they notice you losing hand after hand, and your stack dwindling rapidly, they are going to fancy their chances against you. Every time you make a bet, they will pressurize you by raising. So deny them the opportunity by simply folding all your hands until your luck improves.

Beware

Never, ever, move to a no-limit table in an attempt to recoup your losses quickly. While you can get lucky and win it all back in one or two good hands, remember why you're in this situation in the first place – the cards are not falling for you. If your luck's out, a no-limit table is the last place to be.

171

The World Series of Poker (WSOP)

This is the richest and most prestigious series of poker tournaments in the world. Held annually at the Rio-All Suite Hotel and Casino in Las Vegas, it represents the Holy Grail for all serious poker players.

The World Series of Poker began in 1971 and in that year the championship winner took home $30,000. In 1991, the prize money hit $1,000,000, and since then has continued to rocket. The event is a series of tournaments covering all the main poker games, such as Texas Hold'em, Omaha, Stud, and the various versions, such as Razz and Lowball.

Buy-ins, typically, range from $1000 to $5000, but for the main event – the championship tournament – the buy-in is $10,000. The game in this event is Texas Hold'em, and in 2008 there were 6844 entrants for this one event alone. When you consider that the 2004 event attracted 2500 entrants, you can see how popular it is becoming.

One of the great things about the WSOP is that it is possible to reach the finals without having to put up the huge entry fees. Both the 2003 and 2004 winners qualified via low buy-in satellite tournaments. In recent years, the majority of the finalists have got there via satellites. Indeed, in the 2008 finals, one thousand Poker Stars qualifiers competed in the main event and 123 of them cashed-in, winning more than $9,000,000 between them.

All the tournaments are knock-outs, which is one reason they have proved to be so attractive to the TV channels. The astronomical level of the prize money is another factor.

The winners of the various tournaments are awarded a gold bracelet (which many players value more than the cash prize). The prizes are, typically, in six figures with the first place prize for the 2008 championship being the second highest ever at just over $9,000,000.

Hot tip

In the 2008 WSOP finals, there were over 50 separate tournaments. The main event was the $10,000 buy-in Texas Hold'em tournament.

Should you fancy your chances of taking the huge prize money on offer, or feel you would simply enjoy the experience, there are two ways to participate in the final stages.

The first is to simply stump up the $10,000 necessary to "jump the queue". Having done so, simply turn up in Vegas on the day and your seat will be waiting for you.

For those whose pockets are less deep, the route will be more protracted and difficult – this is the satellite. Basically, satellites are tournaments in which players pay a smaller buy-in for the chance to earn a seat at a larger tournament. This in turn leads to an even larger tournament and so on.

WSOP satellites can be found at both online and live poker rooms. Online, however, is where you'll find the best deals and choice. Online WSOP satellite buy-ins can be as low as $1.00; in fact, some sites even offer freerolls where the prize is a cash buy-in to the next satellite.

Fairly obviously, however, the lower the buy-in, the lower down the chain you are. The more satellites you have to win, the less your chances are of making it to the finals. Your starting point is dependant on what level of buy-in you are prepared to pay. Start at, say, a $500 satellite and you will have a much greater chance of getting there.

Poker satellites offer something quite unique in this competitive world. They give absolutely anyone a chance of competing directly against the very best players. You may be fairly handy with a golf club or tennis racket but there's no way you're ever going to play against Tiger Woods or Roger Federer. That's not the case with poker, though.

Hot tip

The following list shows how the prize money for the main event of the WSOP has escalated over the years:

1971 –	$30,000
1976 –	$220,000
1980 –	$385,000
1985 –	$700,000
1990 –	$805,000
1995 –	$1,000,000
2000 –	$1,500,000
2002 –	$2,000,000
2003 –	$2,500,000
2004 –	$5,000,000
2005 –	$7,500,000
2006 –	$12,000,000
2007 –	$8,000,000
2008 –	$9,000,000

Cheating

Live Poker

In a casino, where all the dealing is done by the dealer, traditional methods of cheating, such as marking the cards and dealing from the bottom of the deck are not possible. But in a non-professional environment, such as the poker party, or a quick game in the lunch break, they certainly are.

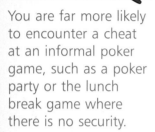

However, there are other ways of cheating in a casino. The most simple is looking at an opponent's cards should he/she be silly enough to let you. The most common is player collusion, which is where two or more players act in unison to the disadvantage of an opponent.

There are several methods used here. One is known as "whipsawing", where two players will raise and re-raise a single opponent to intimidate him/her into folding what is usually the best hand. Another is signalling to each other their intentions or whether they have a really good hand, etc. There are any number of ways this can be done. For example, physical motions, the way chips are handled or stacked, etc. However, this can be a risky business as it is very easy to get seen doing it.

Chip dumping is also quite common. This usually occurs in tournaments where players with large stacks have a definite advantage over those who don't. This form of cheating is where one of the colluders deliberately loses all his chips to his partner, thus doubling his stack. Chip dumping can also be used to keep a partner in a game by giving him chips when his stack is running low.

Online

Cheating in online poker rooms can be done in several ways. Chip dumping, for example, is just as easy to do here as in a live casino and it does go on.

Players can communicate with each other by telephone or instant messaging, the latter being an ideal method as it costs nothing and is impossible to detect.

Alternatively, the colluders can be playing on separate computers in the same room.

It is also quite possible for a single player to set up two or more accounts and aliases, and use them to occupy several seats at the same table. This is effectively the same as two or more colluders working in tandem. The big advantage to someone who does this is that he gets to see dead cards that the opposition don't. For example, say he has 6-6 in one hand and K-6 in another. With one of the two cards he needs to hit trips dead, he'll fold whereas without this knowledge, he'd have played the hand.

Also found online are pokerbots. These are software programs that are programmed to play poker with no input from the owner. Anyone with a rudimentary knowledge of computer programming can set up a pokerbot to play textbook-perfect poker. The bot can either be left to play entirely on its own or just guide its owner's actions, advising on when to bet, fold, etc.

While it's debatable whether the average bot plays any better than the average human, they do offer one big advantage. This is the fact that they do not make the mistakes a human will – a bot will never go on tilt, make bad calls due to lack of concentration or tiredness, or misread a hand.

While on the subject of bots, it must also be said that it's not only players who use them. Many poker rooms use them as well to create the impression they are busy and well used sites. We could mention many names but we won't as we don't particularly want to be sued.

However, you can identify these sites quite easily by comparing them to the well known sites, such as Poker Stars, Party Poker and Ladbrokes. If you come across a site you've never heard of and it has a comparable number of tables running (or even more), you can be sure that the majority of the "players" are, in fact, pokerbots.

Hot tip

Are pokerbots something to worry about? In our opinion, no. They don't play any better than humans; indeed many of them play much worse.

Don't forget

The Internet is a great resource for poker players. You will find hundreds of sites that provide tips and strategies for all the poker games.

Hot tip

There are several different types of poker software available on the Internet. These include programs that provide analysis, odds and probability statistics, and game simulation. Nearly all these programs can be downloaded in "free trial" versions that allow them to be evaluated. Try a few out.

Poker Resources

As poker is a hugely popular game, there are numerous books, magazines and websites devoted to it. The following is a list of recommended reading matter on this subject:

Books

"Theory of Poker" by David Sklansky – this is generally regarded as being the definitive work on poker, and is one that all serious poker players should read. Note that it is not intended for beginners.

"Super/System II" by Doyle Brunson – an updated version of a poker classic. Well worth reading for the section on no-limit Texas Hold'em.

"Hold'em Excellence" by Lou Krieger – this book provides an excellent step-by-step description on how to play each stage of a hand in Texas Hold'em.

"Tournament Poker for Advanced Players" by David Sklansky – one of the best books on tournament play.

Websites

www.cardplayer.com – this is the website of Card Player magazine, and from here you can access over 100 editions of this popular and informative poker publication.

www.poker1.com – website of the well-known poker writer, Mike Caro. Here you will find an extensive range of poker articles and resources.

www.texasholdem-poker.com – a complete resource for the poker player. Strategies, articles, poker tools (odds calculators, for example) are all here.

www.pokerineurope.com – this site is mainly for players in Europe, not surprisingly, and has many articles, details of European tournaments, a shop, and a poker forum.

Poker Forums
www.thepokerforum.com
www.cardschat.com
www.pokerforums.org

Advertise – you advertise by adopting a different style of play in order to confuse your opponents. The usual procedure is to play more loosely, so that when you get a good hand opponents are more likely to call your bets, thus putting money in the pot.

Ante – a small forced bet at the beginning of a hand to ensure money goes into the pot. In online games, it is used in Seven-Card Stud.

All-in – when players puts *all* their chips into the pot, they are said to be all-in. This can happen in any game, but is more commonly seen in no-limit games where it is a powerful maneuver.

American Airlines – pocket aces (A-A). Also known as pocket rockets.

Backdoor – catching both the turn and the river card to complete a drawing hand, usually a straight or a flush.

Bad Beat – holding a really good hand only to have it beaten by an even better one. A typical example would be a full house being beaten by a four-of-a-kind.

Belly Buster – another term for an inside straight where an inside card is needed to complete the hand, e.g. a K with A-Q-J-T.

Beer Hand – 2-7 off suit; the worst start cards in Texas Hold'em. When you're dealt these, it's time to go and have a beer.

Big Blind – a full-sized forced bet made by the player two places to the left of the dealer button.

Bluff – a bet that is made to try and convince opponents that the player has a much stronger hand than is actually the case.

Board – the community cards: flop, turn and river.

Boat – a full house.

Bring-in Bet – a forced bet in Stud poker, typically half of the lower betting limit.

Bubble – the last position in a tournament that doesn't earn any money.

Call – a bet that matches the previous player's bet.

Calling Station – a player who does little else than call, and rarely raises.

Cap – making the last permitted raise in a betting round, usually the fourth.

Chasing – consistently trying to hit unlikely draws. This is a common error.

Check – an action that keeps a player in the game without actually placing money in the pot. This option is available only when a previous player has checked.

Check-Raise – checking, and then raising when the betting comes back round. The raise option will only be available, though, if another player has made a bet.

Collusion – a form of cheating, whereby two or more players collude to gain an advantage over the other players. They communicate by telephone or instant messaging to tell each other what their cards are. They will then use this information to gain an unfair advantage. However, online poker rooms have ways of detecting collusion.

Connector – two cards that are next to each other in rank, e.g. 9-8.

Counterfeit – this is when a card that ruins a good hand falls on the board. For example, a player is holding A-9 and the board is 5-6-7-8. The player has a straight. Then the river brings a 9. Now everyone has the same straight. The player's hand has been counterfeited.

Dead Card – a card needed by a player to complete a hand, but that is already in play, and thus unavailable.

Dominated Hand – a hand that is similar to another hand but with a lower kicker. For example, A-J dominates A-8 because A-8 needs to improve to at least a pair in order to win. If neither hand improves, A-J will win.

Door Card – the first card dealt face-up in Seven-Card Stud.

Double Up – double your chip stack in one hand. This is usually the result of a successful all-in bet in no-limit Hold'em.

Drawing Dead – attempting to hit a hand that will lose even if it completes. For example, you have 5-6-7-8 and an opponent has T-J-Q-K. If a 9 comes to complete your straight it will complete a higher straight for your opponent.

Drawing Hand – a hand that needs one or more cards to make a complete hand, e.g. A-2-3 needs 4-5 to complete a straight.

Extra Blind – a forced bet made by a player joining a table. The purpose is to prevent players skipping from table to table to avoid paying the blind money.

Fish – a weak player.

Flat Call – this is when a player calls with a strong hand, instead of raising.

Flop – the first three community cards in Texas Hold'em.

Flush – a five-card hand in which all the cards are the same suit.

Flush Draw – a hand made up of the same suit but needing more cards of that suit to complete a flush.

Fold – the act of discarding a hand.

Four-of-a-Kind – a hand containing four cards of the same rank, e.g. Q-Q-Q-Q. Commonly known as "quads".

Gutshot Straight – a straight draw that needs an inside card to complete it: e.g. 4-5-7-8, which needs a 6. Also known as an inside straight.

Heads-Up – a term used to describe a situation when two players are contesting the pot. It is also used to describe a two-seat table.

Hit – a term used when players have caught a card, or the hand, they wanted. For example, "the flop hit" or "you hit your hand".

Hole Cards – the initial cards dealt to a player at the beginning of a hand. Also known as pocket cards.

Inside Straight Draw – four cards that need one in the middle to complete a straight. Also known as a gutshot straight.

Kicker – a card used to determine the winner in a situation when two or more players have the same hand. For example, Player A has 7-7 with an ace kicker and Player B has 7-7 with a queen kicker. Player A has the highest kicker and wins the pot.

Limp – a term for a player who enters a pot by calling the bet made by the big blind.

Loose – a style of play adopted by many beginners in which far too many hands are played. Loose players are generally regarded as the easiest ones to beat.

Made Hand – a hand that can win without any improvement, i.e. a pair of aces.

Maniac – a very loose and aggressive player who does a lot of raising and bluffing. These players can be dangerous opponents when the luck is with them, but solid players will always beat them eventually.

Muck – to discard a hand without revealing it to opposing players. In a live poker room, the muck is the pile of folded cards on the table.

Multi-way Pot – a pot that is being contested by several players.

No-Limit – a variation on the standard form of fixed-limit poker, in which players are not restricted in terms of the size of bet they can make.

Nuts – a hand that cannot be beaten with the board as it stands. The term is also used when a player has the best hand of a particular type, e.g. a nut straight or a nut flush.

Off-Suit – a hand containing cards of different suits. For example, 2s-8c.

One-Gap Connector – two cards that are two ranks apart. For example, K-J is a one-gap connector. 5-2 is a two-gap connector.

Out – this is a card needed by a player to complete a hand. For example, if a ten is needed then there are four outs (four tens in the pack).

Overcard – this is a card higher than any on the board. If you are holding 7-J and the flop is T-8-3 then you have one overcard.

Overpair – a pair that is higher than any board card. If you have T-T and the board cards are 9-3-8, the T-T is an overpair.

Pocket Cards – a player's face-down cards that opponents cannot see.

Pocket Pair – a pair in a player's pocket cards.

Post – placing a forced bet on the table, e.g. "posting the small blind".

Pot Odds – the ratio between the amount of money in the pot and the size of the bet needed to call the previous bet. The figure is used to determine if making a bet is likely to be profitable.

Protecting a Hand – the act of making a bet (a raise, usually) to force opponents to fold.

Quads – a term that describes a four-of-a-kind, e.g. K-K-K-K.

Rags – a set of very poor cards that are unplayable.

Rainbow – a set of cards of different suits that cannot be made into a flush. A flop of As-Jd-8h is a rainbow flop.

Rake – a percentage of the pot taken by the poker room as its profit.

Rank – the strength of a card or a hand. For example, a king is a high-ranked card and a two is a low-ranked card. A flush is a high-ranked hand while a pair is a low-ranked hand.

Represent – an act of deception in which a player attempts to make opponents think he or she has a particular hand. For example, if the flop brings a king, a player who immediately raises would be "representing" a good hand containing at least another king.

Ring Game – any poker game that is not a tournament.

River – the last community card in Texas Hold'em. It is also the final card dealt in Seven-Card Stud.

Runner – a turn or river card that completes a player's hand. If it's both then it becomes a "runner runner", e.g. a runner runner straight.

Sandbagging – another term for slow-playing.

Scare Card – a community card that could turn a winning hand into a losing one. For example, a third card of the same suit falling on the board makes a flush a possibility. A player holding a straight would be "scared" by this card.

Semi-Bluff – this is when a player aggressively plays a weak hand that has the potential to become a very strong hand. A flush or straight draw is a typical example. The player hopes that by doing this the other players will fold. However, if they don't, there is still a chance of improving the hand and winning the pot anyway.

Set – another term for a three-of-a-kind.

Short-Stack – a term used when a player is running out of chips, i.e. "short-stacked".

Showdown – the final stage in a hand when all the players still in have their cards turned face-up.

Side pot – when a player goes all-in, a side pot is created for other players. The all-in player is eligible only for the main pot.

Sixth Street – the sixth card dealt in Seven-Card Stud.

Slow-Playing – an act of deception designed to trick opponents into thinking a player has a poor hand, and thus enticing them to put money in the pot.

Small Blind – the lower of the two blind forced bets. The player immediately to the left of the dealer has to post the small blind.

Smooth-Calling – another term for slow-playing. Instead of raising with a big hand, a player will just call to keep opponents in the game.

Steal the Blinds – the act of raising pre-flop to make everyone fold, and thus take the pot there and then.

Steel Wheel – a straight flush – A-2-3-4-5.

Sucker Straight – also known as "Idiot End". This is when a player has hit the low end of a straight and an opponent has hit the high end.

Suited Connector – connected cards of the same suit, e.g. Ks-Qs.

Tell – an indication given unwittingly by a player holding a strong hand that gives the fact away. Online, tells are restricted to the speed at which players act.

Three-Betting – making the third bet in fixed-limit Texas Hold'em. For example, Player A makes a bet and Player B raises. If Player C re-raises, this player is three-betting.

Three-Quarter – this is when a player holds both the best high and the best low hands in a Hi/Lo game. Another player also holding one of these hands can only win a quarter of the pot, and is said to have been "three-quartered".

Tilt – players go on tilt when they lose control of their emotions. In this situation their play becomes irrational, and as a result they lose their stack quickly.

Top Kicker – a hand with the highest possible kicker. For example, a pair of kings with an ace.

Top Pair – a pair containing the highest card on the board. If a player is holding K-9 and the board cards are 8-2-K, the player has the top pair.

Trapping – an act of deception in which a good hand is slow-played to "trap" an opponent into thinking he or she has a better hand.

Trips – another term for a three-of-a-kind.

Turn – the fourth community card in Texas Hold'em and Omaha.

Under the Gun – the player to the left of the big blind. This player is the first to act, and is therefore said to be "under the gun".

Underdog – this term describes a player against whom the odds are stacked. Statistically, this player has more chance of losing than of winning.

Underpair – a pair that is lower than any card on the board. For example, a player has 3-3 and the board is showing 6-K-9.

Up-card – a card that is part of a player's hand, which the other players can see. Up-cards are seen in Stud poker.

Wheel – a term for the best possible low-hand in Seven-Card Stud Hi/Lo and Omaha Hi/Lo – A-2-3-4-5.

Whipsawing – when two players will raise and re-raise a single opponent to intimidate him/her into folding.

Wrap – in Omaha, a starting hand containing four cards of consecutive rank, e.g. 2-3-4-5.

Zone – a player who's making all the right moves is said to be in the "zone".

A

Advertise	177
Aggression	76
All-in bet	84, 88, 92, 154, 160, 177
Analyze your game	165
Ante	126, 177
Atlantic City	9

B

Backdoor	177
Backdoor straight draw	71
Bad beat	166, 177
Bankroll	95
Beer hand	177
Belly buster	177
Blackjack	9
Blacklist	99
Blacklisted casinos	97
Blind	24
Attacking from	58
Big	24
Defending	57
Playing from	57
Posting	24
Small	24
Stealing	56, 57–58, 155
Bluffing	47–48, 89
In no-limit poker	89
In short-hand poker	78
Reasons to	47–48
When not to	48
Board	24, 178
Boarded two-pair	64
Boat	178
Bubble	178
Buggy software	96
Building the pot	44
Burn	168
Busted-out	154

Busting-out	148
Buy-in	91, 146, 150
Buying position	45

C

Calling station	178
Cap	17, 178
Card Player magazine	176
Cash-out procedure	97
Cashback	98
Casino	9, 172, 174
Cheating	
Chip dumping	174
Collusion	174–175, 178
Live poker	174
Marking the cards	174
Multiple accounts	175
Online	174–175
Whipsawing	174, 186
Check	178
Check-raise	37, 46, 159
Checking	37
Check option	25
Chips	147, 152
Chip sets	12
Community cards	24, 106
Computer programming	175
Concealed set	28, 66
Connector	54
Counterfeit	118, 179
Crazy Pineapple	168
Credit card	94

D

Dead card	179
Dealer button	24, 126
Dealing the flop	24
Dealing the river	25

Dealing the turn 25
Deception
  Playing bad hands 49
  Using tells 50
Dominated hand 90, 179
Door-card 126
Double-up 88, 154, 179
Drawing dead 179
Drawing hands 33, 72
  Pot odds 72

E

Electronic funds transfer 97
Extra blind 179

F

Face-up card 129
Fish 22, 95, 180
Five-Card Draw poker 168
Five-card hand 107
Fixed-limit poker
  Betting structure 17
Fixed-limit Texas Hold'em 51–80, 172
  Common pre-flop mistakes 59
  Playing the flop 60–61
    Evaluating the situation 60
    Playing a complete hand 73
    Playing a flush or straight 73
    Playing a full house 75
    Playing flush draws 68–69
    Playing from the blinds 57–58
    Playing overcards 74
    Playing pairs 62–63
    Playing sets 66–67
    Playing straight draws 70–71
    Playing two pairs 64–65
  Playing the river 77
  Playing the turn 76
  Pre-flop play
    Early position 53–54
    Late position 55–56
    Middle position 54–55
  Start cards 24, 52
  The rules 24
Flat call 180
Flop cards 24
Flush draws
  The danger of 29
Four-of-a-Kind 30
Free card
  Buying 45
  Giving away 45
Free poker lessons 9

G

Gaining information 45, 67
Gaming watchdog 97
Gutshot straight 180

H

Handling losing streaks 170
Hand history 96, 165
Hand odds
  Calculating 41
  Table of 43
Heads-up 163
High-limit table 95
High rollers 99
Hole cards 180

I

Identifying dangerous opponents 21–22
Identifying weak opponents 22
Implied odds 42, 72
Inside the mind of a pro 38
Instant messaging 174
Internet 97, 176

J

Joker   168

K

Keeping records   164
Kicker   31, 62, 131, 181

L

Ladbrokes   97, 102, 175
Las Vegas   9, 172
Letting go   92
Limiting the competition   44
Limp   181
Losing streaks   170–171
Low-end straight   70
Lowball   168, 172
Luck   40

M

Maniac   20, 21, 36, 155, 160
Micro-limit table   95
Muck   127, 181
Multi-way pot   77, 181

N

Neteller   97
No-limit poker
    The dangers of   16
No-limit Texas Hold'em   81–92
    All-in bet   88
    Bluffing
        Being caught bluffing   89

Common mistakes   92
Post-flop strategy   87
Pre-flop tips   84–86
Raising   84
Start cards   83
Nut hand   116, 182

O

Off-suit   182
Omaha   26, 106–124, 146, 149, 172
    Common mistakes   124
    Counterfeiting   118
    Hand values   106
    Low hand   109
        Determining the strength of   109
        Qualification   115
        Start cards   112
    Playing the flop   119–121
    Playing the turn and the river 122–123
    Pre-flop strategy   116
    Reading the board   117
    Scooping the pot   109, 122
    Split pot   109
    Start cards
        Evaluation   108–109
        High-hand   110–111
        Low-hand   112–115
        Recommended   114
        Table of   114
    Three-quartered   120
Omaha Eight   106
Omaha Hi/Lo   106
One-gap connector   182
Online poker   10, 93–104
    Bonus   98–99
        Happy hour   99
        Loyalty   98
        Player   99
        Points   99
        Sign-up   98
        Time limit   98
    Cashing in   97
        Anti-fraud checks   97

Jackpot
  Bad-beat 99
  Royal flush 99
Play-money tables 162
Player notes 101
Pros & cons 94, 100
  Accessibility 100
  Anonymity 101
  Choice 100
  Multi-tabling 101
  Playing aids 100
Software 96
  Options 96
Top poker rooms
  Ladbrokes 102
  Party Poker 104
  Poker Stars 103
On the button 116
Open set 67
Other poker games 168
Outs 41, 182
  Table of 43
Overcards 32, 61–62, 74
Overpair 182

P

Pairs 27
Paradise Poker 97
Party Poker 97, 104, 175
Picking the right opponents 19–20
Playing styles 36
  Loose-aggressive 36
  Loose-passive 36
  Tight-aggressive 36
  Tight-passive 36
Playing the flop
  Flop considerations 60
Playing the percentages 40–43
Play and pray hands 63
Pocket cards 24, 182
Pocket pair 182
Pokerbots 175

Poker analysis software 165
  Poker Tracker 165
Poker forums
  www.cardschat.com 176
  www.pokerforums.org 176
  www.thepokerforum.com 176
Poker hand rankings
  Flush 26
  Four-of-a-kind 26
  Full house 26
  Pair 26
  Royal flush 26
  Straight 26
  Straight flush 26
  Three-of-a-kind 26
  Two pairs 26
Poker hand values
  Flushes 29
  Full houses 30
  Pairs 27
  Sets 28
  Straights 28–30
  Two pairs 27
Poker party 11, 174
Poker professional 38, 169
Poker rooms 10
Poker sessions 165
Poker simulation software 163
  Turbo Texas Hold'em 163
Poker software 96, 176
Poker Stars 19, 97, 153, 172, 175
Poker table
  Fold-away 12–13
  Printed Cover 11
Poker websites
  www.cardplayer.com 176
  www.poker1.com 176
  www.texasholdem-poker.com 176
Pot-limit poker
  Betting structure 17
Pot odds 41, 71–72, 80, 183
Practice 162
Pre-flop 24
  Mistakes 59
Prize pool 146, 150

Q

Quads	30
Quality of the opposition	
Determining	19

R

Rags	183
Rainbow	183
Raising	44–45
Raising war	77
Rake	9–10, 183
Rakeback	98
Razz	26, 168, 172
Represent	183
Resources	176
Reverse-bluff	90
Ring game	183
Rio-All Suite Hotel and Casino	172
Rock	36, 154
Roulette	9
Runner	183

S

Sandbagging	184
Semi-bluff	184
Servers	96
Session statistics	96
Set	28
Concealed	66
Open	67
Slow-playing	67
Seven-Card Stud	125–144, 149
Betting structure	126
Bring-in bet	126, 178
Dead cards	129
Door-card	126, 130
Factors specific to	128–129
Fifth Street	127
Fourth Street	127
Live cards	129
Playing flush draws	139
Playing killer hands	143–144
Playing pairs	131
Playing sets	134
Playing straight draws	141
Playing two pairs	137
Seventh Street	127
Sixth Street	127
Spread betting	126
Start cards	130
The rules	126–127
Third Street	126
Up-cards	131
Short-hand poker	78
Blinds	
The effect of	78
Bluffing	78
Drawing hands	78
Short-stacked	91
Showdown	25, 184
Shuffling shoe	13
Side pot	18, 88, 184
Six-seat tables	22
Slot Machines	9
Slow-playing	46, 59, 184
Smooth-calling	184
Split pair	27
Stack	16, 18
Stack Size	91
Stack v pot considerations	18
Steel wheel	185
Straight	28–29
High-ended	28
Inside	28
Low-ended	28
Outside	28
Straight draw	29
Backdoor	71
Straight Flush	30
Stud	172
Sucker straight	185
Suited connector	54
Switching gears	49–50

T

Table image	89
Table position	
Early	34
Late	35
Middle	34
Relative	20
Tells	37, 101, 185
Online	37
Ten-seat table	53
Texas Hold'em	23–38
Specific hand probabilities	80
Start card probabilities	79
Three-quartered	120
Tilt	166, 175, 185
Tournament	103, 145–160, 172
Add-on	148
Blinds structure	147, 157
Bounty feature	151
Freeroll	146, 150
Heads-up	146, 149
Strategy	159–160
Level	147
Lists	146
Lobby	153
Money-paying position	152
Multi-table (MTT)	146–147
Strategy	154–156
Private	146, 149
Prize money	151
Rebalancing	147
Rebuy	146, 148
Periods	148
Satellite	146, 148
Single-table (STT)	146, 149
Advantages of	149
Strategy	157–158
Sit-and-go	146
Super-satellite	148
Televised	146
Tournament director	14
Trapping	86, 90, 154, 185
Trips	28, 186
Turn card	25, 186
TV channels	172
Two-pair	
Boarded	64
Split	65
Two Pairs	27

U

Ultimate Bet	97
Under-betting	92
Underdog	186
Underpair	186
Under the gun	186
Up-card	186

W

Where to play	9–11
Where to sit at the table	20
Wild-card	168
Winning streaks	170
Win expectations	169
World Series of Poker (WSOP)	172–173
Prize money	173
Wrap	186

Z

Zone	186